THE PRAYERS OF SAINT SARAPION

ST VLADIMIR'S SEMINARY PRESS
Popular Patristics Series
Number 65

The Popular Patristics Series published by St Vladimir's Seminary Press provides readable and accurate translations of a wide range of early Christian literature to a wide audience—students of Christian history to lay Christians reading for spiritual benefit. Recognized scholars in their fields provide short but comprehensive and clear introductions to the material. The texts include classics of Christian literature, thematic volumes, collections of homilies, letters on spiritual counsel, and poetical works from a variety of geographical contexts and historical backgrounds. The mission of the series is to mine the riches of the early Church and to make these treasures available to all.

The Prayers of
SAINT SARAPION
The Bishop of Thmuis

A Revised Greek Text and Translation
of the *Euchologion Sarapionis*

Text, Translation, and Introduction by
Maxwell E. Johnson

ST VLADIMIR'S SEMINARY PRESS
YONKERS, NEW YORK
2023

Publisher's Cataloging-in-Publication
(Provided by Cassidy Cataloguing Services, Inc.).

Names: Serapion, of Thmuis, Saint, author. | Johnson, Maxwell E., 1952– translator.

Title: The prayers of Saint Sarapion the Bishop of Thmuis : a revised Greek text and translation of the 'Euchologion Sarapionis' / text, translation, and introduction by Maxwell E. Johnson.

Other titles: Euchologion. English | Euchologion Sarapionis.

Description: Yonkers, NY : St Vladimir's Seminary Press, [2023] | Series: Popular patristics series; 65. | Includes bibliographical references. | Prayers in Greek with English translation.

Identifiers: ISBN: 978-0-88141-752-4 (paperback) | 978-0-88141-753-1 (Kindle) | LCCN: 2023938529

Subjects: LCSH: Serapion, of Thmuis, Saint. Euchologion. English. | Orthodox Eastern Church. Euchologion--History and criticism. | Catholic Church. Sacramentary--History and criticism. | Prayers, Early Christian--History and criticism. | Liturgies, Early Christian--History and criticism. | Liturgics--History--Early church, ca. 30-600. | Sacramentaries--Texts. | Worship-- History--Early church, ca. 30-600. | Holy Spirit--Early works to 1800. | Theology--History-- Early church, ca. 30-600. | BISAC: RELIGION / Christian Rituals & Practice / Sacraments. | RELIGION / Christian Rituals & Practice / Worship & Liturgy. | RELIGION / Christian Theology / Pneumatology.

Classification: LCC: BV185 .S4713 2023 | DDC: 264/.014036--dc23

ST VLADIMIR'S SEMINARY PRESS
575 Scarsdale Road, Yonkers, NY 10707
1-800-204-2665 | www.svspresss.com

ISBN: 978-0-88141-752-4 (paperback) | 978-0-88141-753-1 (Kindle)

PRINTED IN CANADA

For Paul F. Bradshaw
Director, Mentor, and Colleague

Contents

Preface

This new and shorter edition of the *Euchologion* or Prayers of St Sarapion of Thmuis, while based upon my much larger, and now almost thirty-years old, *The Prayers of Sarapion of Thmuis: A Literary, Liturgical, and Theological Analysis*,[1] should not be seen as a replacement for that work. Rather, although reflecting updated scholarship on Sarapion's prayers and correcting previous errors in both the Greek text and the English translation, this edition should be viewed more as an updated summary of that larger work, the continued value of which will be evident throughout this version.

This particular edition owes its genesis to two conversations. First, Coptic Orthodox Bishop Kyrillos Abdelsayed suggested to me some time ago doing a shorter, affordable, and more easily accessible version of Sarapion's *Euchologion*. Second, at the same time, after my 2017 publication of St Cyril of Jerusalem's *Lectures on the Christian Sacraments* in the Popular Patristics Series

[1] Maxwell E. Johnson, *The Prayers of Sarapion of Thmuis: A Literary, Liturgical, and Theological Analysis*, Orientalia Christiana Analecta 249 (Rome: Pontificio Istituto Orientale, 1995).

of St Vladimir's Seminary Press,[2] Fr Ignatius Green and I entered into conversation about doing the Prayers of Sarapion for the same series, which I am pleased to say has now become a reality.

Here let me add as well my profound thanks to Jaroslaw Dziewicki, the managing editor of Orientalia Christiana Analecta, for his kind permission to use in this volume the Greek text and English translation, as well as some quotations, from my previous study. Thanks go also to Professor Nathan Chase at Aquinas Institute of Theology, St Louis, Missouri, for his numerous suggestions in terms of bibliography and content, and for his careful reading of the document.

It should be noted as well that the Eucharistic Liturgy from Sarapion's *Euchologion* has actually been adapted for use in contemporary Greek Orthodox liturgical practice, occurring for the first time in 2013 in the Holy Church of Panagia Myrtioditissa in Piraeus, Greece, with the approval of Metropolitan Seraphim of Piraeus.[3]

[2]St Cyril of Jerusalem, *Lectures on the Christian Sacraments: The Procatechesis and the Five Mystagogical Catecheses ascribed to St Cyril of Jerusalem*, ed. and trans. Maxwell E. Johnson, Popular Patristics Series 57 (Yonkers, NY: St Vladimir's Seminary Press, 2017).

[3]See https://www.johnsanidopoulos.com/2013/06/the-divine-liturgy-of-serapion.html. The text of this Liturgy is available. See *Η Θεία Λειτουργία κατά τον μακάριον πατέρα ημών Σεραπίωνα επίσκοπον Θμούεως: Λειτουργικόν Αυγουσταμνικής της Αιγύπτου*, ed. Pavlos G. Alexas (Athens: EPTALOFOS A.B.E.E., 2013). Unfortunately, the scholarship referred to in the Introduction (see pages 9–18) is seriously out of date.

Whether this is a sign of things to come in liturgical renewal and reform with regard to this and other ancient liturgies (e.g., that of "St James, the brother of the Lord")[4] in the Orthodox Church, including the *versus populum* position of the priest during the anaphora and separate distribution of Christ's Body and Blood, rather than the use of the liturgical spoon to distribute Holy Communion, is still unknown at this time.

March 21, 2023
Commemoration of St Sarapion of Thmuis

[4]For a recent edition of the Liturgy of St James intended for liturgical use, with an introduction that takes into account recent scholarship and provides translations (a revision of Johann von Gardner's Slavonic translation and an English translation) based upon the best extant manuscripts, see Бж҃ественнаѧ литꙋргі́и ст҃а́гѡ ап҃ла ї҆а́кѡва, бра́та гд҇нѧ: Слꙋже́бникъ/*The Divine Liturgies of the Holy Apostle James, Brother of the Lord: Service Books*, ed. and trans. Vitaly Permiakov (Jordanville, NY: The Printshop of St Job of Pochaev, 2021).

Introduction

St Sarapion (or Serapion),[1] bishop of Thmuis (*ca.* 339–360),[2] was a friend of both St Antony the hermit and St Athanasius, the great patriarch of Alexandria. According to Athanasius, Antony often confided in Sarapion about the contents of his visions, and upon Antony's death in 356, Sarapion received one of his two sheepskin garments, with the other going to Athanasius (*Vita Antoni*

[1]The variant spellings of his name come from similar variations in the Greek manuscripts of the works of Athanasius of Alexandria. Since the dominant form in those manuscripts is Σαραπίων (*Sarapiōn*), and since the two occurrences of his name within the thirty prayers ascribed to him also use Σαραπίων, this work uses *Sarapion* unless directly citing an author using the variant spelling.

[2]Thmuis (the modern day Timay el-Amdid) is located in Lower Egypt between the Mendesian and Tannatic branches of the Nile River, south of Lake Menzaleh. While there were two cities in Egypt with the name of Thmuis, only this Thmuis in Lower Egypt had its own succession of bishops. On Thmuis and its bishops, both orthodox and heretical, see Giorgio Fedalto, *Hierarchia Ecclesiastica Orientalis*, II: *Patriarchatus Alexandrinus, Antiochenus, Hierosolymitanus* (Padua: Messaggero, 1988), 611.

82 and 91).[3] To Sarapion, Athanasius addressed the eleventh of his Festal Letters (*ca.* 339),[4] a letter *Ad Serapionem de morte Arii* (*ca.* 358),[5] and his important *Epistulae IV ad Serapionem episcopum Thmuitanum* (*ca.* 359–360) on the Holy Spirit.[6]

According to Athanasius in *Ad Draconitum* 7 (*ca.* 354–355),[7] Sarapion himself had been a monk and had presided as an abbot over a monastic community before becoming bishop of Thmuis. Jerome notes that he was given the name "Scholasticus" because of his great learning (*De viribus illustribus* 99).[8] And the fifth-century Byzantine historian Sozomen writes that this "prelate distinguished by the wonderful sanctity of his life and the power of his eloquence" was sent by Athanasius with four other Egyptian bishops and three presbyters to the court of Constantius in 356 "to conciliate the emperor; to reply, if requisite, to the calumnies of the hostile [Arian] party; and to take such measures as they deemed most advisable for the welfare of the Church and himself."[9] While the date and circumstances of his death are unknown, Jerome says that during the reign

[3]PG 26:957 and 971 (NPNF² 4:217 and 220).

[4]PG 26:1412–14 (NPNF² 4:538–39).

[5]PG 25:685–90 (NPNF² 4:564–66).

[6]PG 26:529–676; ET in *The Letters of St. Athanasius Concerning the Holy Spirit*, trans. C. R. B. Shapland (London: The Epworth Press, 1951), 58–189.

[7]PG 25:523 (NPNF² 4:559).

[8]PL 23:700 (NPNF² 3:380).

[9]Sozomen, *Ecclesiastical History* 4.9 (NPNF² 4:497).

of Constantius, Sarapion was exiled from his see and suffered as a "confessor."[10] The commonly accepted date of Athanasius' *Epistulae IV ad Serapionem episcopum Thmuitanum* (*ca.* 359–360) suggests that his death would have occurred after 360, and Quasten dates it sometime "after 362." In the Coptic Orthodox Church, a martyr by the name of Sarapion is commemorated on March 7, but elsewhere, at least in the Byzantine and Roman Rites, March 21 is the commemoration of Sarapion of Thmuis. The *Roman Martyrology* says simply "*In Aegypto, sancti Serapiónis, anchorétae*" ("In Egypt, St Serapion, anchorite," i.e., hermit).[11]

Very few of Sarapion's writings are extant.[12] While Jerome (*De viribus illustribus* 99) refers to an *egregius liber* ("excellent book") called *Against the Manichees*, a work on titles of the Psalms, and "valuable epistles to various persons," only *Against the Manichees*,[13] two letters in Greek (*Ad monachos* and *Ad Eudoxium*),[14] one letter to the disciples of Antony on the occasion of his

[10]Jerome, *De viribus illustribus* 99 (NPNF[2] 3:380).

[11]*Martyrologium Romanun* (Vatican City: Libreria Editrice Vaticana, 2001), 188.

[12]See Klaus Fitschen, *Serapion von Thmuis, Echte und unechte Schriften sowie die Zeygnisse des Athanasius und Anderer*, Patristische Texte und Studien 37 (Berlin: DeGruyter, 1992).

[13]Robert Pierce Casey, *Serapion of Thmuis: Against the Manichees*, Harvard Theological Studies 15 (Cambridge, MA: Harvard University Press, 1931), 29–78.

[14]Sarapion, *Ad Eudoxium episcopum* (PG 40:923–926); *Ad monachos* (PG 40:925–42).

death (preserved only in Syriac and Armenian translations),[15] an Arabic *Life of Antony*,[16] and a few fragments (i.e., *Ep.* 23,[17] *Ep.* 55,[18] a *Letter to Confessors*,[19] and a commentary on Genesis[20]) survive. Beyond these extant writings, Socrates relates a short saying attributed by Evagrius to "Serapion, the angel of the church of the Thmuïtae"[21] (HE 4:23), which Alban Butler called "a short epigram or summary of Christian perfection which he often repeated: 'the mind is purified by spiritual knowledge (or by holy meditation and prayer), the spiritual passions of the soul by charity, and the irregular appetites by abstinence and penance.'"[22] And, of course,

[15] R. Draguet, "Une lettre de Sérapion de Thmuis aux disciples d'Antoine (A.D. 356) en version syriaque et arménienne," *Le Muséon* 64 (1951): 1-25. "There existed at one time," notes Johannes Quasten "a collection of as many as twenty-three letters" (*Patrology*, III: *The Golden Age of Greek Patristic Literature from the Council of Nicea to the Council of Chalcedon* [Utrecht/Antwerp, 1966] 84).

[16] See Elizabeth Agaiby, *The Arabic* Life of Antony *Attributed to Serapion of Thmuis: Cultural Memory Reinterpreted*, Texts and Studies in Eastern Christianity 14 (Leiden: Brill, 2019).

[17] PG 96:512a.

[18] PG 96:481d–484a.

[19] Jean Baptiste Pitra, *Analecta sacra Spicilegio solesmensi parata*, 4 (Paris: Typis Tusculanis, 1883), 214–15.

[20] Robert Devreesse, ed., *Les anciens commentateurs grecs de l'Octateuque et des Rois*, Studi e Testi 201 (Vatican City: Biblioteca apostolica vaticana, 1959), 181.

[21] Socrates, *Ecclesiastical History* 4.23 (NPNF[2] 2:108).

[22] *Butler's Lives of the Saints*, vol. 1, ed. and rev. H. J. Thurston and D. Atwater (London: Burns & Oates, 1956), 656. The current edition of *Butler's Lives of the Saints*, New Full Edition, March, rev. Teresa

the collection of prayers, euchologion, or sacramentary, explicitly names Sarapion as author in the title of Prayer 1 (Εὐχὴ Προσφόρου Σαραπίωνος ἐπισκόπου, *Euchē Prosphorou Sarapiōnos episkopou*) and in the title before the title of Prayer 15 (Προσευχ Σαραπίωνος θμούεως, *Proseuch Sarapiōnis Thmoueōs*).

The thirty prayers ascribed to St Sarapion in the eleventh-century, or twelfth-century[23] Greek manuscript located in the library of the Monastery of the Great Lavra on Mount Athos (MS. Lavra 149) were first discovered and published by A. Dimitrievskij in 1894,[24] and shortly thereafter by Georg Wobbermin in 1898.[25] The edition with which most students in the English-speaking world were familiar in the past, however, was published in 1900 by F. E. Brightman, who, thinking that the prayers were out of sequence in the manuscript, rearranged

Rodriguez (Collegeville, MN: The Liturgical Press, 1999), 220, incorrectly lists "St. Serapion, martyr at Alexandria (first century)" for March 21, and incorrectly cites the *Roman Martyrology* as the source.

[23]See H. Brakmann "ⲂⲀⲠⲦⲒⲤⲘⲀ ⲀⲒⲚⲈⲤⲈⲰⲤ: Ordines und Orationen kirchlicher Eingliederung in Alexandrien und Ägypten," in "*Neugeboren aus Wasser und Heiligem Geist*": *Kölner Kolloquium zur Initiatio Christiana*, ed. H. Brakmann, Tinatin Chronz, and Claudia Sode (Münster: Aschendorff Verlag, 2020), 85–196.

[24]A. Dimitrievskij, *Ein Euchologium aus dem 4. Jahrhundert, verfasst von Sarapion, Bischoff von Thmuis* (Kiev, 1894).

[25]Georg Wobbermin, *Altchristliche liturgische Stucke aus der Kirche Aegyptens nebst einem dogmatischen Brief des Bischofs Serapion von Thmuis* (Leipzig and Berlin: J. C. Hinrichs, 1898).

them according to what he considered to be their logical order.[26]

BRIGHTMAN'S RE-ORDERING *Numbers after each prayer corresponding to the manuscript order*	ORDER OF THE PRAYERS IN MS LAVRA 149
1. First Prayer of the Lord's Day (19)	1. Prayer of Offering of Bishop Sarapion
2. Prayer after the Standing Up after the Homily (20)	2. Fraction after the Prayer....
3. Prayer for the Catechumens (21)	3. Laying on of Hands after Giving of…
4. Laying on of Hands on the Catechumens (28)	4. Prayer after Distribution...
5. Prayer for the People (27)	5. Prayer for Those Offering Oils/Water
6. Laying on of Hands on the People (29)	6. Laying on of Hands after blessing....
7. Prayer for the Sick (22)	7. Sanctification of Waters
8. Laying on of Hands on the Sick (30)*	8. Prayer for Those Being Baptized
9. Prayer for Fruit-bearing (23)	9. Prayer after the Renunciation
10. Prayer for the Church (24)	10. Prayer after the Reception
11. Prayer for the Bishop and the Church (25)	11. Prayer after Being Baptized…
12. Prayer of Genuflexion (26)	12. Laying on of Hands...Deacons
13. Prayer of Offering of Bishop Sarapion (1)	13. Laying on of Hands… Presbyters
14. Fraction after the Prayer and Prayer	14. Laying on of Hands...Bishop during the Fraction (2)

[26]Frank Edward Brightman, "The Sacramentary of Serapion of Thmuis," *Journal of Theological Studies* 1 (1900): 88–113, 247–77. This rearrangement includes the insertion of Prayers 15 and 16 (prayers for the prebaptismal and postbaptismal oils) into Prayers 7–11 (the baptismal prayers) and a complete re-ordering of Prayers 19–30 (the so-called "preanaphoral" prayers).

15. Laying on of Hands of the People after the Giving of the Fraction to the Clergy (3)	15. Prayer(s) of Sarapion, Bishop Prayer for the Oil of… Baptized
16. Prayer after the Distribution of the People (4)	16. Prayer for the Chrism… Annointed
17. Prayer for Those Offering Oil and Water (5)	17. Prayer for the Oil of Sick (Bread, Water)
18. Laying on of Hands after the Blessing of Oil and Water (6)	18. Prayer for One Who Has Died….
19. Sanctification of Waters (7)	19. First Prayer of the Lord's Day
20. Prayer for Those Being Baptized (8)	20. Prayer after Homily
21. Prayer after the Renunciation (9)	21. Prayer for Catechumens
22. Prayer after the Reception (10)	22. Prayer for the Sick
23. Prayer after Being Baptized and Coming Up (11)	23. Prayer for Fruit-bearing
24. Laying on of Hands for the Appointment of Deacons (12)	24. Prayer for the Church
25. Laying on of Hands for the Appointment of Presbyters (13)	25. Prayer for the Bishop and-Church
26. Laying on of Hands for the Appointment of a Bishop (14)	26. Prayer of Genuflexion
27. Prayer(s) of Sarapion, Bishop of Thmuis, Prayer for the Oil of Those Being Baptized (15)	27. Prayer for the People
28. Prayer for the Chrism... (16)	28. Laying on of Hands for Catechumens
29. Prayer for the Oil of the Sick or for Bread or Water (17)	29. Laying on of Hands of the People
30. Prayer for One Who Has Died and Is Being Carried Out (18)	30. Laying on of Hands on the Sick*

*After this prayer the manuscript says: "All these prayers are to be accomplished before the Prayer of Offering."

Brightman's text and order were followed by F. X. Funk in his 1905 edition[27] and by Johannes Quasten in 1935,[28] with the unfortunate result that Brightman's rearranged order was often treated as though it represented the original shape of the text. This was also the order followed in modern French versions.[29] While English versions of some of these prayers appeared in various collections of texts, the only complete English translation of all thirty was first made by John Wordsworth from Wobbermin's edition in 1899, which he further revised on the basis of Brightman's text in 1923.[30] Even though Wordsworth similarly thought that the prayers were out

[27]Francis Xavier Funk, *Didascalia et Constitutiones Apostolorum*, vol. 2 (Paderborn: Ferdinand Schoeningh, 1905), 158–95.

[28]Johannes Quasten, *Monumenta eucharistica et liturgica vetustissima* (Bonn: Hanstein, 1935), 135–57.

[29]See André Hamman, *Prières des premiers chrétienes* (Paris: Arth. Fayard, 1952), and Lucien Deiss, *Aux sources de la liturgie* (Paris: Editions Fleurus, 1963). The English versions appearing in the translations of André Hamman, *Early Christian Prayers*, trans. Walter Mitchell (Chicago: Henry Regnery Co., 1961), 117–31, and Lucien Deiss, *Springtime of the Liturgy*, trans. Matthew J. O'Connell (Collegeville, MN: The Liturgical Press, 1979, repr. 1991), 97–134, are based on the French translations rather than directly on the Greek text.

[30]John Wordsworth, *Bishop Sarapion's Prayer Book: An Egyptian Pontifical Dated Probably About A.D. 350–356* (London: Society for Promoting Christian Knowledge, 1899; 2nd ed. 1923; repr. Hamden, CT: Archon Books, 1964). A little known anonymous English translation of Prayers 19–30 and 1–6 appears in Thomas A. Michels, ed., *Blessed Mysteries: Liturgical Prayers Attributed to Bishop Serapion of Thmuis* (Keyport, NJ: St. Paul's Priory, 1945).

of order in the manuscript, he printed them according to the order in which they appear. More recently, both John Barrett-Lennard and I prepared English editions that followed the order of Lavra MS 149.[31] This volume continues that approach, while providing both a corrected Greek text and English translation from my earlier edition.

[31] R. J. S. Barrett-Lennard, *The Sacramentary of Sarapion of Thmuis: A Text for Students, with Introduction, Translation, and Commentary* (Bramcote, Nottingham: Grove Books, 1993); Maxwell E. Johnson, *The Prayers of Sarapion of Thmuis.*

i. Survey of Scholarship

Leading to my work on the prayers ascribed to Sarapion, first as my 1992 doctoral dissertation at the University of Notre Dame, under the direction of Paul F. Bradshaw, who graciously gave me the handwritten research notes of Geoffrey Cuming for my use,[1] and then in a subsequent monograph in the Orientalia Christiana Analecta series,[2] there had been no scholarly consensus on the order, date, authorship, nature, theology, and liturgical context of this document. Of the numerous articles and studies that appeared within the past century and one half of scholarship,[3] significant essays by Bernard Capelle,[4] Bernard Botte,[5] and Geoffrey Cuming[6] merit particular attention as determining and representing

[1]These are the notes Cuming used to prepare his "Thmuis Revisited: Another Look at the Prayers of Bishop Sarapion," *Theological Studies* 41 (1980): 568–75.

[2]See p. ix, note 1. I gave it the title of "Prayers" simply because these appear as titles in the collection itself.

[3]The first work to treat this text in some detail was P. Drews, "Über Wobbermins 'Altchristliche liturgische Stücke aus der Kirche Agyptens,'" *Zeitschrift für Kirchengeschichte* 20 (1900): 291–328, 415–41.

[4]Bernard Capelle, "L'anaphore de Sérapion: essai d'exégèse," *Le Muséon* 59 (1946): 425–43; reprinted in idem, *Travaux liturgiques de doctrine et d'histoire*, vol. 2 (Louvain: Abbaye du Mont-César, 1962), 344–58, from which it is cited here.

[5]B. Botte, "L'Eucologe de Sérapion est-il authentique?" *Oriens Christianus* 48 (1964): 50–56.

[6]Geoffrey J. Cuming, "Thmuis Revisited: Another look at the prayers of Bishop Sarapion," *Theological Studies* 41 (1980): 568–75.

the parameters of the previous debate. It was Capelle's opinion, based on the repetition of certain words and phrases appearing both in the anaphora or "Prayer of Offering of Bishop Sarapion" (Prayer 1) and in other prayers,[7] that the entire document was to be viewed as a single, unified, literary work written by a single author from a particular theological perspective. According to him, while one may find vestiges of traditional Egyptian liturgical forms and prayers throughout the text, these traditional elements were not introduced without drastic modifications. The most important indication of this

[7] Such words and phrases include: τῇ γενητῇ φύσει (*tē genētē physei*) with ὁ πάσῃ τῇ γενητῇ φύσει (*ho pasē tē genētē physei*) in Prayer 7; διερμηνευόμενον τοῖς ἁγίοις (*diermēneuomenon tois hagiois*) with ἡμῖν ... διερμηνεύειν (*hēmin ... diermēmeuein*) in Prayer 19; πάτερ ... χορηγὲ τῆς ἀθανασίας (*pater ... chorēge tēs athanasias*) with τὸν θεὸν ... χορηγὸν πάσης εὐλογίας in Prayer 25; διὰ τῆς ἐπιδημίας (*dia tēs epidēmias*) with διὰ τῆς ἐπιδημίας τοῦ ἀρρήτου σου λόγου (*dia tēs epidēmias tou arrētou sou logou*) in Prayer 7; ἐπιδημίας (*epidēmias*) with τὸ πνεῦμα τῆς ἀληθείας ἐπιδημήσῃ αὐτῷ (*to pneuma tēs alētheias epidēmēsē autō*) in Prayer 13; θεὲ τῆς ἀληθείας (*thee tēs alētheias*) with similar titles of God in Prayers 2, 8, 9, 11, 14, 15, 21, and 27; αἷμα τῆς ἀληθείας (*haima tēs alētheias*) with ἐκταθῆναι τὴν τῆς ἀληθείας χεῖρα (*ektathēnai tēn tēs alētheias cheira*) in Prayer 3; φάρμακον ζωῆς (*pharmakon zōēs*) with εἰς φάρμακον ζωῆς (*eis pharmakon zōēs*) in Prayer 17 and other occurrences of φάρμακον (*pharmakon*) in Prayers 5 and 30; νοσήματος (*nosēmatos*) with ἐπιτίμησον τοῖς νοσήμασιν (*epitimēson tois nosēmasin*) in Prayer 22; πᾶσαν προκοπὴν (*pasan prokopēn*) with προκοπήν (*prokopēn*) and εὐλογίαν προκοπῆς (*eulogian prokopēs*) in Prayer 25 and εἰς προκοπήν (*eis prokopēn*) in Prayer 3; and ἀρετῆς (*aretēs*) with πλήθυνον ἐν ἀρετῇ καὶ πίστει (*plēthynon en aretē kai pistei*) in Prayer 19.

modification, according to Capelle, is the epiclesis of the Logos both upon the baptismal waters in the "Sanctification of the Waters" (Prayer 7) and upon the eucharistic gifts in the anaphora (Prayer 1). Such invocations, combined with a lack of emphasis upon the Holy Spirit in the oil prayers (Prayers 15–17), display "a suspect tendency of attributing to the Logos the role others assigned to the Holy Spirit."[8] Furthermore, he claimed that there was no evidence for an epiclesis of the Logos in the Alexandrian liturgical tradition before Sarapion in *ca.* 350 and that later Egyptian sources (e.g., Peter II of Alexandria and Theophilus of Alexandria) assume the epiclesis of the Holy Spirit as a traditional element. All of this suggested to him that Sarapion was the first and only one to create an epiclesis of the Logos, an epiclesis that, while in harmony with the economic trinitarian theology of Athanasius reflected in his *Letters to Sarapion on the Holy Spirit,* was, nevertheless, ultimately his own innovative work without any parallels elsewhere. Capelle's conclusions were firm and precise: "An epiclesis of the Logos at Alexandria before 350 is a phantom. At Thmuis it was a reality, but one which was owed, without doubt, to the good pleasure and innovative genius of Bishop Serapion."[9] For Capelle, then, the value of Sarapion's text as an authoritative witness to the early Egyptian liturgical tradition was extremely limited. It represented, rather, one individual's innovative use of that tradition to produce a

[8]Capelle, "L'anaphore de Sérapion," 355.

[9]Capelle, "L'anaphore de Sérapion," 355–56.

unique text consistent with his own theological position and approach.

While Capelle never suggested reasons why a fourth-century Egyptian bishop might take this particular theological approach in distinction to what he considered to be the received tradition, it was Bernard Botte's influential opinion that the reasons were to be discovered in the fact that the document was not the work of Sarapion of Thmuis at all but represented a deliberate Arianizing or Pneumatomachian redaction dating from a half to an entire century later. This tendency was demonstrated, he believed, by the text's trinitarian theology. The word ἀγένητος (*agenētos*), appearing with an "astonishing frequency" in the prayers, is applied exclusively to the Father, and suggests the Arian opposition between the "uncreated" Father and the "created" (γενητός, *genētos*) Son. While γενητός (*genētos*) does not appear anywhere in the text as a description of the Son, Botte saw this Arianizing approach confirmed by the opposition between ἀγένητος (*agenētos*) and ὑπόστασις (πάσῃ γενητῇ ὑποστάσει) (*hypostasis* [*pasē genētē hypostasei*]) in reference to creation in the preface of the anaphora.[10] Furthermore, the Son is called λόγος (*logos*) seven times and μονογενής (*monogenēs*) or μονογενής υἱός (*monogenēs hyios*) forty-seven times, but there is no "allusion to the divinity of the Son nor to his equality with the Father."[11] This subordinationism of

[10]Botte, "L'Eucologe de Sérapion," 52–53.
[11]Botte, "L'Eucologe de Sérapion," 53.

the Son is matched, Botte believed, by a similar subordinationism of the Holy Spirit. Noting that πνεῦμα ἅγιον or ἅγιον πνεῦμα (*pneuma hagion, hagion pneuma*) appears thirty-nine times in the text "always without the definite article" (*toujours sans article*), except in Prayer 16 where it functions as the liturgical formula for "confirmation" (sic!), that παράκλητος (*paraklētos*) never occurs, and that πνεῦμα θεῖον (*pneuma theion*) appears in the prayers for the ordination of presbyters (Prayer 13) and the bishop (Prayer 14), Botte stated that "one has the impression that the author considered the Holy Spirit as an impersonal force rather than a divine person."[12]

Botte found this conclusion supported by what he claimed was the consistent use of the un-coordinate form of the doxology (still orthodox in 350–60?), by the absence of the Holy Spirit in the oil prayers (a silence "more eloquent than a declaration"), and especially by the epicleses of the Logos in the anaphora (Prayer l) and the blessing of the baptismal waters (Prayer 7). Rather than an innovator, who represented an economic trinitarian theology that could be considered orthodox, therefore, "Pseudo-Sarapion" was a heretic who intentionally substituted the Logos for the Holy Spirit wherever he could. "This is not an archaic doctrine of the Holy Spirit. It is a deliberate attempt to put the Holy Spirit in the shade. This is not very likely on

[12]Botte, "L'Eucologe de Sérapion," 53–55.

the part of the real Serapion, who provoked the letters of St Athanasius on the divinity of the Holy Spirit."[13]

Geoffrey Cuming offered significant challenges to the conclusions of both Capelle and Botte, as well as to the Brightman-Funk rearrangement of the prayers. Along with a suggestion made by Theodor Schermann in 1912,[14] but originally independently of him,[15] Cuming contended that the order of the prayers in the manuscript is logical, if one assumes that the eleventh-century Athonite copyist began his work on the reverse side of the manuscript roll with the anaphora rather than on the front with Prayer 15, where, significantly, this prayer is prefaced by a general title, possibly intended for the entire document, Προσευχ Σαραπίωνος θμούεως (*Proeuch Sarapiōnos Thmoueōs*). Realizing his mistake the copyist appended the note that all of the prayers, presumably 19–30, were to be accomplished prior to the anaphora (Πᾶσαι αὗται εὐχαὶ ἐπιτελοῦνται πρὸ τῆς εὐχῆς τοῦ προσφόρου, *Pasai hautai euchai epitelountai pro tēs euchēs tou prosphorou*), thus giving rise to the hypothesis that Prayers 19–30 are to be viewed as pre-anaphoral. The only other prayer that has a

[13]Botte, "L'Eucologe de Sérapion," 55.

[14]Theodor Schermann, "Abendmahlsgebete im Euchologium des Serapion," in *Aegyptische Abend mahlsliturgien des ersten Jahrtausends in ihrer Oberlieferung dargestellt, Studien zur Geschichte und Kultur des Altertums* 6.1–2 (Paderborn: Schöningh, 1912) 102–103.

[15]Cuming made no reference to Schermann in "Thmuis Revisited," but did cite him in his *Liturgy of St Mark,* Orientalia Christiana Analecta 234 (Rome: Pontifical Oriental Institute, 1990), xxxvii.

title attributing authorship is the anaphora—Εὐχὴ Προσφόρου Σαραπίωνος ἐπισκόπου (*Euchē Prosphorou Sarapiōnos episkopou*)—and Cuming noted that a similar style of euchological composition (where a general title appears at the beginning of the Liturgy and a subordinate one appears at the head of the anaphora) is "paralleled most relevantly in the Liturgy of St. Mark in the Coptic version."[16] With the assumption of this eleventh-century copying mistake, therefore, the contents of the document have the following logical order: Preliminary Blessings of Oils (Prayers 15-17); A Burial Prayer (Prayer 18, the oldest prayer of its kind); The Eucharistic Liturgy (Prayers 19–30 and Prayers 1–6); Baptismal Prayers (Prayers 7–11); and Ordination Prayers (Prayers 12–14).[17]

Against Capelle's claim that the document is a homogenous literary piece, Cuming argued that there was textual evidence for claiming that it was composed of different strata or various groups of prayers. Taking a suggestion made by Brightman in an appendix to his edition that, on the basis of vocabulary (words present and absent) and literary style (e.g., the unique use of a verb of prayer followed by ὥστε [*hōste*]), Prayers 15–18 form an independent group, Cuming analyzed

[16]For this to be an exact parallel, however, the "general title" in Sarapion's prayers would have to come before Prayer 19, the first of the so-called "pre-anaphoral" prayers, and not before the baptismal oil prayers.

[17]Cuming, "Thmuis Revisted," 570.

these prayers further and concluded that only Prayers 15–17 should be considered as making up this unit.

> To the curious idiom with *hoste*, the strongest point of all, may be added the titles of these three prayers, which all begin *Euche eis...*, whereas all other titles use *meta* (indicating sequence), *hyper, peri,* or straight genitive. Unconscious quirks of style such as this are the most reliable indicators of authorship.[18]

This conclusion, however, was reached some eighty years earlier by Paul Drews, who had argued that Prayers 15–17 represent revisions of earlier prayers for the baptismal oils and the oil for the sick, just as the anaphora represents a revision of an earlier eucharistic prayer.[19]

Cuming, however, went further. Expanding his literary analysis to include other prayers in the collection, he continued:

> Two further examples may be adduced which suggest the existence of different strata within the collection. Of the nine preanaphoral prayers (19–27), six use the word *gnosis;* the same six also use the word *katharos,* not a common word in liturgy. Neither of these words occurs in the anaphora, but both occur also in the ordination

[18] Cuming, "Thmuis Revisited," 572.

[19] Drews, 300ff. Cuming demonstrated no familiarity with this earlier work, and Brightman, "The Sacramentary of Serapion," 277, merely alluded to it in a different context.

> prayers. *Logos* occurs in the anaphora and in three of the five baptismal prayers, but nowhere else in the collection.[20]

Against Botte's thesis that the entire text is reflective of a conscious heretical theological position, Cuming also appealed to the letters of Athanasius, where the Holy Spirit and the Logos are closely connected.

> For Athanasius an epiclesis of the Logos necessarily involves the Spirit also. The first half of the fourth century did not make the sharp distinction between Logos and Pneuma which we take for granted. On this count, at any rate, Sarapion can claim to be completely orthodox.[21]

Similarly, against Botte's charge of subordinationism based on the Arian contrast between the Father as ἀγένητος (*agenētos*) and the Son as μονογενής (*monogenēs*), he noted that: (1) ἀγένητος (*agenētos*) is often confused with ἀγέννητος (*agennētos*) in texts and the loss of a *nu* could easily have been an error on the part of the copyist; (2) the appropriate Arian distinction is between ἀγένητος and γενητός (*agenētos, genētos*), a distinction that the text nowhere makes; and (3) the description of the Father as γεννήτωρ τοῦ μονογενοῦς (*gennētōr tou monogenous*) in Prayer 20 offers possible, if conjectural, support for ἀγέννητος (*agennētos*) as the original reading elsewhere in the document.[22]

[20]Cuming, "Thmuis Revisited," 572.
[21]Cuming, "Thmuis Revisited," 573.
[22]Cuming, "Thmuis Revisited," 574.

With Sarapion's "orthodoxy" and, thereby, the traditional dating of the text thus vindicated, Cuming sought additional support from the anaphora. By analyzing those sections that have parallels in the Greek and Coptic anaphoras of St Mark,[23] he argued that "Sarapion knew an earlier and simpler form of the anaphora of St. Mark than that of the *textus receptus*."[24] He saw this primarily in: (1) the introduction to the Sanctus, which omits any reference to the cherubim and, like that of the Der Balizeh papyrus, refers to the seraphim covering the "face" rather than the "faces," as in both versions of St Mark; (2) the offering language of the post-Sanctus epiclesis, which, while probably intended to be consecratory, "shows traces of an older conception of the sacrifice of praise, not otherwise known later than the second century";[25] and (3) the shorter form of the institution narrative in comparison to other sources of St Mark. He therefore concluded that:

[23]For a text of Greek St Mark in English see Paul F. Bradshaw and Maxwell E. Johnson, *Prayers of the Eucharist: Early and Reformed*, Fourth Edition, (Collegeville: Liturgical Press Academic, 2019), 57–66. For Coptic Mark see F. E. Brightman, *Liturgies Eastern and Western*, vol. 1: *Eastern Liturgies* (Oxford University Press, 1896), 164–80 (hereafter PEER4). See also Cuming, *Liturgy of St Mark*. For the best current overview of the St Mark anaphoral tradition and all the sources see H. Brakmann, "Die alexandrinische Markus-Liturgie und ihre arabische Version im Codex Sinaticus Arabicus 237," in *La Liturgie de S. Marc dans le Sinaï Arabe 237, Édition et traduction annotée*, ed. Ugo Zanetti (Münster: Aschendorff Verlag, 2021), 9–40.

[24]Cuming, "Thmuis Revisited," 575.

[25]Cuming, "Thmuis Revisited," 574.

> If the text of Sarapion's anaphora was further revised at a later date, it is most probable that the opportunity would have been taken to update the sections from St. Mark to conform with their latest version at Alexandria. It thus becomes increasingly possible that the collection and editing of these prayers was, after all, the work of Sarapion, Bishop of Thmuis, the friend of Athanasius.[26]

Previous scholarship, as represented by these three approaches, therefore, was one of confusion and contradiction. Sarapion's euchologion may have been a homogenous literary work or an edited collection of diverse strata. It may have been an authoritative witness to the early Egyptian liturgical tradition or, alternatively, so reflective of an individual theological agenda that any attempt to deduce that tradition is doomed to failure from the start. It may have been an early or mid-fourth-century text or dated much later. And, as such, it may have been reflective of either an orthodox theological position or a later Semi-Arian Pneumatomachian one. In my own work on these prayers, I have taken the three approaches of Capelle, Botte, and Cuming as offering a threefold methodology for the possible resolution of these contradictions: (1) literary analysis; (2) liturgical analysis; and (3) theological analysis.

[26]Cuming, "Thmuis Revisited," 575.

ii. Literary Analysis

On the basis of both vocabulary and style, Drews, Brightman, and Cuming all suggested that Prayers 15–17 represented one literary stratum of the document, an independent prayer-group that was incorporated into the text's final shape. I applied this same kind of literary analysis to the rest of the document, and noted that other strata or groups of prayers are also suggested. Three examples must suffice here: the baptismal prayers, the ordination prayers, and six of the so-called pre-anaphoral prayers. In the baptismal group (Prayers 7–11) the use of the particle ὅπως (*hopōs*) in two of them (7 and 8), the presence of an articular infinitive in three of them (7, 8, and 9), the use of μηκέτι (*mēketi*) followed by ἀλλά (*alla*) in four of them (7, 8, 9, and 11), and other parallel or common elements discerned among all five of them, suggest that the baptismal group of prayers represents a separate stratum in the document, coming either from a common baptismal source and euchological tradition or from an author using stylistic devices different from those discerned in Prayers 15–17. This becomes all the more striking when one considers that both Prayers 7–11 and 15–16 are prayers designed for the various rites of Christian initiation.

Similarly, analysis of the three ordination prayers (Prayers 12–14) suggests that these prayers for the deacons and the bishop belong to yet another literary stratum, as the following comparative chart demonstrates:

PRAYER 12 (DEACONS)	PRAYER 14 (BISHOP)
ὁ τὸν… ἀποστείλας…	ὁ τὸν… ἀποστείλας…
ποιμνίων,	ποίμνην…
ὁ ἐκλεξάμενος ἐπισκόπους….	
ὁ ἐκλεξάμενος διὰ…	ὁ δι'… ἐκλεξάμενος… ἐπισκόπους…
κατάστησον καὶ τόνδ διάκονον…	Ποίησον… καὶ τόνδε ἐπίσκοπον
καὶ δὸς ἐν αὐτῷ πνεῦμα…	καὶ δὸς αὐτῷ… πνεῦμα…
καθαρῶς καὶ ἀμέμπτως	ἀμέμπτως καὶ ἀπροσκόπως
διακονῆσαι ἐν τῇ λειτουργίᾳ	ἐν τῇ ἐπισκοπῇ διατελείτω
ταὐτῇ.	
ho ton… aposteilas…	*ho ton… aposteilas…*
poimniōn,	*poimnēn…*
ho eklexamenos episkopous…	
ho eklexamenos dia…	*ho di'… eklexamenos… episkopous*
katastēson kai tone diakonon…	*Poiēson… kai tonde episkopon*
kai dos en autō pneuma….	*kai dos autō… pneuma…*
katharōs kai amemptōs	*amemptōs kai aproskopōs*
diakonēsai en tē leitourgia	*en tē episkopē diateleitō.*
tautē.	

When Prayer 13, the prayer for the ordination of presbyters, is compared with these, some significant differences are revealed. First, instead of an introduction referring to God's activity in sending the Son and through Him choosing the orders of ministry, this prayer begins by referring directly to the imposition of hands on this (τοῦτον, *touton*) candidate. Second, rather than an imperative formulaic-sounding statement "appointing"

or "making" the candidate a presbyter, Prayer 13 simply and uniquely prays (δεόμεθα ἵνα, *deometha hina*) for the Spirit to come. In fact, this is the only occurrence in the entire document where a verb of prayer is followed immediately by an ἵνα (*hina*) clause. Even when an analogous use of a second-person imperative occurs in reference to the gift of the Spirit for the carrying out of the respective ministries, this prayer uses μέρισον καὶ τῷδε πνεῦμα ἅγιον (*merison kai tōde pneuma hagion*) instead of something like δὸς ἐν αὐτῷ πνεῦμα (*dos en autō pneuma*). Third, in further reference to the Spirit, Prayer 13 uses γενέσθω (*genesthō*), the third-person aorist imperative form of γίνομαι (*ginomai*), a form that rarely appears elsewhere in the document.[1] Fourth, only this prayer uses an articular infinitive (πρὸς τὸ δύνασθαι αὐτὸν οἰκονομῆσαι, *pros to dynasthai auton oikonomēsai*). And, finally, Prayer 13 uses the verb ὑπηρετέω (*hypēreteō*), a verb that appears elsewhere in the text only in Prayer 9. Therefore, while a case can be made for Prayers 12 and 14 belonging together, the differences noted in Prayer 13 suggest that it may represent not only a different stratum or origin but even a different theology of ordination itself, as essentially

[1]It occurs elsewhere only in Prayers 7, 27, and 30. In Prayer 7 it refers to the coming of the Logos into the baptsmal waters (ὁ ἀρρητός σου λόγος διὰ τῆς ἐπιδημίας ἐν αὐτοῖς γενέσθω, *ho arrētos sou logos dia tēs epidēmias en autois genesthō*) and so appears as a close parallel to the epicletic intent of Prayer 13.

an imposition of hand and prayer for the Spirit rather than an imperative "appointing" or "making"!

As noted above, Cuming suggested that in six of the nine so-called pre-anaphoral prayers—namely, Prayers 19, 21, 24, 25, 26, and 27—another literary stratum might be discerned. While he made his suggestion only on the basis of the common occurrence of γνῶσις (*gnōsis*) and καθαρός (*katharos*), other minor correlations between these prayers may add further cumulative support to his hypothesis: εὐεργετέω or εὐεργέτης (*euergeteō*, *euergetēs*) in Prayers 19, 26, and 27; ἄγγελος or ἀγγελικός (*angelos*, *angelikos*) in Prayers 19, 24, and 27; μανθάνω or μάθημα (*manthanō*, *mathēma*) in Prayers 19 and 21; the verb βεβαιόω (*bebaioō*) in Prayers 21, 27, and 29; the verb καταργέω (*katargeō*) in Prayers 21, 24, and 26; the same aorist passive form of καταλλάσω (*katallasō*) in Prayers 24 and 27; and the verb συγχωρέω (*synchōreō*) in Prayers 24 and 26.

While they are simply too detailed to be given an adequate treatment here,[2] further verbal and stylistic parallels between the various groups of prayers tend to suggest that the document's final shape is the result of the blending together of four distinct strata:

Group One: Prayers 2–6 (Communion Prayers), Prayers 7–11 (Baptism), Prayer 13 (Ordination of Presbyters), Prayers 19, 21, 24, 25, 26, and 27 (Pre-anaphoral?), and Prayers 28–30 (Blessings);

[2]See Johnson, *The Prayers of Sarapion of Thmuis*, 83–110.

Group Two: Prayers 15–17 (Oils);

Group Three: Prayers 12 and 14 (Ordination of Deacons and the Bishop); and Prayers 20, 22, and 23 (Pre-anaphoral?); and

Group Four: Prayer 18 (Burial).

Regarding Prayer 1 (the prosphora or anaphora), it is important to recall that Capelle's thesis of the document's homogeneity was based on verbal parallels between it and the rest of the document.[3] But the most that can be said is that there may be a literary relationship between the anaphora and *some* of the other prayers. And, with the exception of θεός τῆς ἀληθείας, φάρμακον, and νοσήματος (*theos tēs alētheias*, *pharmakon*, and *nosēmatos*), Capelle's specific parallels are parallels *only* with Prayers 3, 7, 19, and 25, all of which I assign above to Group One. Furthermore, the words ἀγένητος, λόγος, and μυστήριον (*agenētos*, *logos*, and *mystērion*) are also contained *only* in the anaphora and in other prayers belonging to this same hypothetical stratum. The parallels suggested by Capelle, then, simply do not serve as evidence for concluding that this document is a unified literary piece composed by a single author. Alternatively, what they do suggest is that, at some level of its development, the anaphora belonged to those prayers comprising Group One of the text,

[3]See page xvi, note 16.

prayers that generally appear to be representative of a common euchological tradition or style.

On a literary level alone, therefore, it appears that the best description of the contents of the document is, with Cuming's initial hypothesis, that of a collection of various and diverse prayers. And, if this is correct, then the order of the prayers as it appears in the manuscript is logical indeed. As a *collection*, prayers for the Eucharist, Baptism, ordinations, oils, burial, the Liturgy of the Word or daily prayer, and blessings or dismissals are simply and logically grouped together according to the contents, *not* necessarily according to their supposed ritual sequence or order.[4] If this is indeed the case, then there is every reason to accept the suggestions made by both Schermann and Cuming that the original document from which these prayers were copied in MS Lavra 149 began with Prayers 15–17, the prayers that are preceded by the title Προσευχ Σαραπίωνος θμούεως (*Proseuch Sarapiōnos thmoueōs*). Even if, as is customary in some ancient Greek manuscripts, the general title of a work came at the end of a manuscript roll rather than its beginning,[5] the same conclusion is suggested. For, in either case, the document would begin with Prayer 15.

[4]On extant, somewhat parallel Egyptian prayer collections, such as the recently published Ethiopic Aksumite Collection, see Ágnes T. Mihálykó, *The Christian Liturgical Papyri: An Introduction*, Studien und Texte zu Antike und Christentum 114 (Tübingen: Mohr Siebeck, 2019), 40–41, 43–44, and 224–44.

[5]See Eric G. Turner, *Greek Manuscripts of the Ancient World*, 2nd rev. ed. (London: Institute of Classical Studies, University of London, 1987), 14.

The conclusion, however, that Prayers 19–30 should be understood as pre-anaphoral prayers belonging to the Liturgy of the Word at the Eucharist is less certain, and must be accepted with some degree of caution. Since it is known that morning and evening prayer in the "cathedral" office of Lower Egypt contained readings from Scripture,[6] and since the fifth-century Byzantine historian, Socrates, refers to an Alexandrian tradition of Wednesday and Friday *synaxes* "without the celebration of the mysteries,"[7] the possibility is suggested that Prayers 19–30 represent not pre-anaphoral prayers but a *collection* of various prayers from which a selection might be made in different liturgical contexts.[8] Consequently, there is no reason why Prayers 19–30 may not be placed logically at the *end* of the document as they presently occur in the manuscript. While, as noted above, the appended statement by the copyist after Prayer 30—Πᾶσαι αὗται εὐχαὶ ἐπιτελοῦνται πρὸ τῆς εὐχῆς τοῦ προσφόρου (*Pasai hautai euchai epiteluontai pro tēs euchēs tou prosphorou*)—may certainly indicate that the eleventh-century Athonite copyist understood them to be pre-anaphoral; it does not mean necessarily that they were intended to be that by the original editor.

[6]See Robert Taft, *The Liturgy of the Hours in East and West* (Collegeville, MN: The Liturgical Press, 1986), 34–35.

[7]Socrates, *Ecclesiastical History* 5.22.

[8]See Louis Duchesne, *Christian Worship: Its Origin and Evolution*, 5th ed., trans. M. L. McClure (London: Society for Promoting Christian Knowledge, 1920), 79.

iii. Liturgical Analysis

Analysis of the overall liturgical context of the document also suggests that those prayers assigned above to Group One reflect not only a different literary stratum of the document but a chronologically earlier stratum of development as well. Concerning the ordination prayers, for example, Paul Bradshaw suggested that the prayer for presbyters (Prayer 13) with its primary focus on a teaching ministry, may reflect an earlier period in Egyptian liturgical history.

> According to the fifth-century Church historian Socrates, preaching by presbyters at Alexandria was prohibited after the time of Arius (c. 250–c. 336), for fear of the spread of further heresies, and hence this prayer must have originated before that step was taken, or alternatively the situation must have been different at Thmuis or wherever it was composed.[1]

What seems equally significant, however, is the fact that of the three ordination prayers only this one corresponds to the more primitive pattern of ordination rites, where the election of the candidate was followed simply by a prayer for the gifts needed to fulfill that particular office. In the prayers for the deacons and the bishop (Prayers 12 and 14), on the other hand, the use of

[1] Paul Bradshaw, *Ordination Rites of the Ancient Churches of East and West* (New York: Pueblo, 1990), 63.

κατάστητον (*katastēton*, Prayer 12) and ποίησον (*poiēson*, Prayer 14) appears to imply a different and later concept of ordination. Here the emphasis is less on the gifts needed for ministry and more on the prayer itself as that which "gives" the office.

I have suggested strongly that a similar distinction of liturgical strata may be noted between the baptismal prayers (Prayers 7–11) and the pre-baptismal and post-baptismal consecration of oil prayers (Prayers 15–16). Building upon the work of Georg Kretschmar[2] and Paul Bradshaw[3] I have argued that the early Egyptian baptismal tradition, like that argued by Gabriele Winkler for early Syria,[4] had only a pre-baptismal anointing, with a post-baptismal anointing with chrism being introduced in the fourth century.[5] It may be significant

[2]Georg Kretschmar, "Beiträge zur Geschichte der Liturgie, insbesondere der Taufliturgie, in Ägypten," *Jahrbuch für Liturgik und Hymnologie* 8 (1963): 1–54.

[3]Paul Bradshaw, "Baptismal Practice in the Alexandrian Tradition: Eastern or Western?" in Paul Bradshaw, ed., *Essays in Early Eastern Initiation*, Alcuin/GROW Liturgical Study 8 (Nottingham: Grove Books, 1988), 5–17.

[4]See Gabriele Winkler, "The Original Meaning of the Prebaptismal Anointing and its Implications," in Maxwell E. Johnson, ed., *Living Water, Sealing Spirit: Readings on Christian Initiation* (Collegeville, MN: Pueblo, 1995), 58–81; and idem, *Das Armenische Initiationsrituale*, Orientalia Christiana Analecta 217 (Rome: Pontifical Oriental Institute, 1982).

[5]In addition to my *The Prayers of Sarapion*, 124–43, Chapter 2 of my *Liturgy in Early Christian Egypt*, Alcuin/GROW Liturgical Study 33 (Bramcote: Grove Books, 1995), and my "Baptism and Chrismation in Third- and Fourth-Century Egypt," *Worship* 88.4 (2014):

then that, while a pre-baptismal anointing can be placed somewhere in relationship to Prayers 8 and 9 (cf. the use of σφραγίζω [*sphragizō*] in Prayer 9, "Prayer after the Renunciation"), Prayers 7–11 appear to be complete without any postbaptismal anointing.[6] Prayer 11, "Prayer

311–32, see also for the most recent study of baptismal rites, H. Brakmann "ⲂⲀⲠⲦⲒⲤⲘⲀ ⲀⲒⲚⲈⲤⲈⲰⲤ: Ordines und Orationen kirchlicher Eingliederung in Alexandrien und Ägypten." In "*Neugeboren aus Wasser und Heiligem Geist": Kölner Kolloquium zur Initiatio Christiana*, ed. H. Brakmann, Tinatin Chronz, and Claudia Sode (Münster: Aschendorff Verlag, 2020), 85–196. Brakmann's reference to a 2014 essay by Alistair Stewart, "The Early Alexandrian Baptismal Creed: Declaratory, Interrogatory...or Both?" *Questions Liturgique* 95 (2014): 237–53, should be balanced by my more recent essay, "Interrogatory Creedal *Formulae* in Early Egyptian Baptismal Rites: A Reassessment of the Evidence," *Questions Liturgiques* 101 (2021): 75–93.

[6]Based on parallels in a variety of Eastern baptismal rites (e.g., early Syrian, Armenian, Byzantine, and Coptic), including the recently discovered Aksumite baptismal order in Alessandro Bausi, "*Euchologion* from the Aksumite Collection: Translation" (Forthcoming; used with permission), and idem, "The *Baptismal Ritual* in the Earliest Ethiopic Canonical Liturgical Collection," in *Neugeboren aus Wasser und Heiligem Geist*, 31–83. It is possible that some version of Prayer 15 for the consecration of pre-baptismal oil was used in the context of the pre-baptismal anointing itself, as held by Brightman. The consecration of chrism for post-baptismal anointing, however, while appearing as a post-baptismal prayer in the Aksumite baptismal order, does not regularly occur within the baptismal rites of the Christian East, but is done apart from its immediate conferral. But, see *Brakmann,* "ⲂⲀⲠⲦⲒⲤⲘⲀ ⲀⲒⲚⲈⲤⲈⲰⲤ," 121–28 and 136–34, who argues that the original location for oil blessings in Egypt was at the very beginning of the baptismal rite (as in the *Canons of Hippolytus)* and it gradually moved to their pre- and post-baptismal locations during the rite itself, as witnessed to by Aksumite *Euchologion*, with

after Being Baptized and Coming Up," makes no reference to any post-baptismal anointing either preceding it or to follow. It reads, rather, like a final blessing (εὐλόγησον τὸν δοῦλόν σου τοῦτον εὐλογίᾳ τῇ σῇ, *eulogēson ton doulon sou touton eulogia tē sē*) or dismissal prayer to conclude the rite itself. If Prayers 15–17 are a literary unit, therefore, it may well be that they represent the introduction of the post-baptismal anointing (Prayer 16) into the Egyptian tradition, under Syrian influence and the revision of a prayer for the pre-baptismal oil (Prayer 15). Such a distinction has been obscured by the Brightman-Funk placement of Prayers 15–16 within Prayers 7–11 themselves.

Further, while both Kretschmar and Bradshaw suggested that Prayer 15, with its overall emphasis on healing and re-creation, belonged to a period prior to the addition of a post-baptismal anointing, it includes signs of possible revision that might be expected with the introduction of such an anointing. Such signs are: (1) the probable exorcistic connotation of the healing of "satanic taint"; (2) a paschal focus on dying to sin and living to righteousness consistent with a fourth-century

---

the final shift of the consecration of chrism as an altogether separate rite from initiation itself sometime between the 8th and 10th centuries in Egypt. And see Nathan Chase, "Further Reflections on the Post-baptismal Anointing and Handlaying in the Egyptian Initiatory Tradition" (forthcoming). It seems likely, therefore, that Prayers 15 and 16, or an earlier version of each, were used, not within Sarapion's baptismal rite at the location of the respective anointings, but at the very beginning of the rite.

Eastern reinterpretation of Baptism along the lines of Romans 6; and (3) the ritual sequence of anointing-bath-anointing possibly implied in the phrase, "being re-created through this anointing, and being cleansed through the washing, and being renewed in the Spirit ..."[7]

Concerning the anaphora, it has long been assumed that those elements that have parallels to both Greek and Coptic St Mark (i.e., the introduction to the Sanctus, the Sanctus, and the first epiclesis) represent an earlier version of those elements, interpolated from Alexandria into the anaphora at Thmuis. Of major significance here is the reference within the introduction to the Sanctus to the two "most-honored" seraphim who cover the "face" (as in Coptic Mark or Cyril) rather than the "faces," as in St Mark. That these "seraphim" originally referred to the Son and Holy Spirit covering the "face" of *God* in the native Egyptian liturgical and theological tradition and only later were reduced to angels covering their "faces" in the interests of trinitarian orthodoxy was the thesis of Gregory Dix in his 1938 essay, "Primitive Consecration

[7]For a critique of my interpretation of the baptismal rite in Sarapion, though accepting a mid-fourth century date for the prayers in general, see Bryan D. Spinks, "Sarapion of Thmuis and Baptismal Practice in Early Christian Egypt: The Need for a Judicious Reassessment," *Worship* 72 (May, 1998): 255–70, and my response, "The Baptismal Rite and Anaphora in the Prayers of Sarapion of Thmuis: An Assessment of a Recent 'Judicious Reassessment,'" *Worship* 73.2 (March 1999): 140–68.

Prayers."[8] Noting such an interpretation in the *De principiis* of Origen,[9] Dix claimed that the anaphoral Sanctus itself had an Egyptian origin and was known, in essentially the same form as reflected in Sarapion's text, to Origen in Alexandria in the first half of the third century. While Dix's theory of its Alexandrian origins has been questioned,[10] Kretschmar argued that Origen's theology strongly influenced its particular shape and interpretation when it finally came to be added to the Alexandrian anaphoral structure. According to him, this relationship between the Egyptian Sanctus and Origen's theology was so strong that only a bishop influenced by his theology could have introduced it into the anaphora, an event that must have happened in the second half of the third century.[11] And in his own work on the origins and development of the Sanctus, Robert Taft sided with Dix and Kretschmar, writing:

> That the Sanctus in Egypt, when it does appear, shows the characteristics Dix and Kretschmar note

[8]Gregory Dix, "Primitive Consecration Prayers," *Theology* 37 (1938): 261–83.

[9]Origen, *De principiis* 1.3.4; 4.3.14.

[10]See the work of Bryan D. Spinks, *The Sanctus in the Eucharistic Prayer* (Cambridge University Press, 1991), where a Syrian origin is suggested. Also with regard to a Syrian origin see Gabriele Winkler, *Das Sanctus. Über den Ursprung und die Anfänge des Sanctus und sein Fortwirken,* Orientalia Christiana Analecta 267 (Rome: Pontifical Oriental Institute, 2002).

[11]Georg Kretschmar, *Studien zur frühchristlichen Trinitätstheologie,* Beiträge zur historischen Theologie 21 (Tübingen: Mohr Siebeck, 1956), 164.

> in Origen, is clear. It is also evident that the Sanctus is central to the flow of the reworked Egyptian anaphoral structure, and not just a crude interpolation. Kretschmar is certainly right, too, in viewing this Egyptian liturgical setting of the Sanctus as the result of the Judeo-Christian, Alexandrian exegesis of Is 6 adopted and developed by Origen, and in concluding that this influenced the Egyptian anaphoral tradition, and that decisively. But when? That this Sanctus is already in place *ca.* 350 in Sarapion is clear. So just when, in the years between *ca.* 250–350, the Sanctus was actually interpolated into the Egyptian anaphoral structure is by no means clear.... Kretschmar believes already in the third century, and though I am unable to confirm this dating, I also see no reason to challenge it.[12]

I have accepted the conclusions of Dix, Kretschmar, and Taft on the Origenist-Alexandrian origins of the Sanctus in Egypt, as reflected in Sarapion's anaphora.[13]

[12]Robert Taft, "The Interpolation of the Sanctus into the Anaphora: When and Where? A Review of the Dossier: Part II," *Orientalia Christiana Periodica* 58 (1992): 82–121, at 94–95.

[13]Johnson, *The Prayers of Sarapion of Thmuis*, 205–219. See also my "The Archaic Nature of the Sanctus, Institution Narrative, and Epiclesis of the Logos in the Anaphora Ascribed to Sarapion of Thmuis," in Robert F. Taft, ed., *The Christian East, Its Institutions & Its Thought: A Critical Reflection: Papers of the International Scholarly Congress for the 75th Anniversay of the Pontifical Oriental Institute, Rome, 30 May–5 June 1993*, Orientalia Christiana Analecta 251

But, first in his book on the Sanctus[14] and, then, in an article challenging my own work,[15] Bryan Spinks has argued against Dix, Kretschmar, Taft, and me that there is "little justification for seeing the theology of Origen" behind Sarapion's text at all.[16] According to Spinks, Sarapion's reference to the τὰ δύο τιμιώτατα σεραφεὶμ ἑξαπτέρυγα (*ta dyo timiōtata serapheim hexapteryga*) merely reflects an Alexandrian identification of the two living creatures in the LXX version of Habakkuk 3.2 (ἐν μέσῳ δύο ζῴων, *en mesō dyo zōōn*) with the seraphim of Isaiah 6.3, an identification known by both Clement of Alexandria (*Stromateis* 7.12)[17] and Athanasius (*In illud omnia mihi tradita sunt* 6).[18] Consequently:

(Rome: Pontifical Oriental Institute, 1996), 671–702; "The Origins of the Anaphoral Use of the Sanctus and Epiclesis Revisited: The Contribution of Gabriele Winkler and Its Implications," in H.-J. Feulner, E. Velkovska, and R. Taft, eds., *Crossroad of Cultures: Studies in Liturgy and Patristics in Honor of Gabriele Winkler*, Orientalia Christiana Analecta 260 (Rome: Pontifical Oriental Institute, 2000), 405–442; and "Recent Research on the Anaphoral *Sanctus*: An Update and Hypothesis," in Maxwell E. Johnson, ed., *Issues in Eucharistic Praying in East and West: Essays in Liturgical and Theological Analysis* (Collegeville, MN: The Liturgical Press, Pueblo, 2011): 161–88.

[14]Spinks, *The Sanctus in the Eucharistic Prayer* (Cambridge University Press, 1991).

[15]Bryan D. Spinks, "The Integrity of the Anaphora of Sarapion of Thmuis and Liturgical Methodology," *Journal of Theological Studies* 49.1 (1998): 136–44.

[16]Spinks, *Sanctus*, 87.

[17]GCS 17 (ANF 1:546).

[18]PG 25:220 (NPNF[2] 4:90).

> This link, together with the strange petition which introduces the pericope, might suggest to the speculative mind Origen's theology equating seraphim with the Son and Spirit. However, the text does not actually make this equation and is perfectly consistent with the understanding found in Clement and Athanasius that the two living creatures were the seraphim. The thought of the Thmuis eucharistic prayer seems to be: Christ and the Holy Spirit speak in us, so that we, like the living creatures [seraphim] who stand beside you, may praise you with the Holy, holy, holy.[19]

In his more recent essay Spinks refined his position to say that even if the Dix-Kretschmar-Taft approach "remains a conjecture, and requires this [Origenist] exegesis to be read into the anaphoral text," it is, nonetheless, "suggestive and plausible."[20] Similarly, he also modified his position slightly on the "two living creatures," saying that Sarapion's petition (i.e., "Let the Lord Jesus speak in us and let [the] Holy Spirit also hymn You through us") is to be "interpreted more naturally as simply reflecting the indwelling of the Son and Spirit.... We cannot join the heavenly worship unless Christ and the Holy Spirit make their dwelling in us."[21] Even if this interpretation

[19]Spinks, *Sanctus*, 89.
[20]Spinks, "The Integrity of the Anaphora," 141.
[21]Ibid.

might be plausible, the fact is that the text in question *does* say quite clearly that it is the Son and Spirit themselves, who sing *in* and *through* the assembly as they "hymn *God* through us." Hence, indwelling or not, the "heavenly worship" in which the liturgical assembly joins appears to be precisely that which is offered by the Son and Holy Spirit *to* the Father. And this is "perfectly consistent" not with Clement and Athanasius but with Origen, who also knows the traditional equation of the ζῷα (*zōa*) of Habbakuk 3.2 with the two seraphim of Isaiah 6, but nevertheless associates them with the Son and the Holy Spirit.

The unique bi-partite institution narrative in Sarapion's anaphora, separated by the use of *Didache* 9.4, may also be a sign of antiquity.[22] While Dix argued that the *Didache* reference could be omitted as "a rather unimaginative literary quotation" making no sense in the context of the Nile delta,[23] others have seen it as a clue to a more primitive shape of the Eucharistic Liturgy lying behind Sarapion's text. Following the work of Klaus Gamber,[24] Edward Kilmartin argued that Sarapion's separation of the bread and cup words by this citation "probably reflects a former practice in

[22]On this, however, see the forthcoming study of Predrag Bukovec, *Die frühchristliche Eucharistie*, Wissenschaftliche Untersuchungen zum Neuen Testament (Tübingen: Mohr Siebeck, 2022).

[23]Gregory Dix, *The Shape of the Liturgy* (London: Dacre Press, 1945), 167.

[24]Klaus Gamber, "Die Serapion-Anaphora, ihrem altesten Bestand nach untersucht," *Ostkirchliche Studien* 16 (1967): 33–42.

Egypt of introducing the meal between the Eucharistic rites."[25] Louis Bouyer suggested that this structure "leads one to think that it resulted from remodeling found in the 7th book of the *Apostolic Constitutions*."[26] And, while Spinks has claimed that the presence of the *Didache* quotation may be nothing other than the citation of the equivalent of canonical Scripture,[27] Enrico Mazza has argued that Sarapion and this remodeling of the prayers of *Didache* 9 in *Apostolic Constitutions* 7.25 (with a structure consisting of the thanksgiving over the bread, *Didache* 9.4, and the thanksgiving over the cup)[28] are both dependent upon a common "paleo-anaphoric" source. Consequently, while the institution narrative itself may be an addition to an earlier text, its separation of the bread and cup words by *Didache* 9.4 is "a truly unique and exceptional witness to the archaic and pre-anaphoric structure of eucharistic

[25]Edward J. Kilmartin, "Sacrificium Laudis: Content and Function of Early Eucharistic Prayers," *Theological Studies* 35 (1974): 274.

[26]Louis Bouyer, *Eucharist: Theology and Spirituality of the Eucharistic Prayer*, trans. Charles Underhill Quinn (Notre Dame, IN: University of Notre Dame Press, 1968), 208.

[27]See Spinks, "The Integrity of the Anaphora," 142–43.

[28]Enrico Mazza, "L'anafora di Serapione: una ipostesi di interpretazione," *Ephemerides Liturgicae* 95 (1981): 510–28. See also idem, *The Origins of the Eucharistic Prayer*, trans. Ronald E. Lane (Collegeville, MN: Pueblo, 1995), 219–40. For a text in English of the anaphora of *Apostolic Constitutions*, Book 8, see Paul F. Bradshaw and Maxwell E. Johnson, *Prayers of the Eucharist: Early and Reformed*, 51–52.

celebration."[29] This possibility (combined with the fact that Sarapion's institution narrative itself is shorter than all other sources for the Liturgy of St Mark and lacks the characteristically later "addition of verbs and honorific adjectives"[30]) may suggest, therefore, that, rather than being a suspect "innovation," Sarapion's text is an important and potentially reliable witness to the early liturgical tradition. Not only might it point to one early structure of the Eucharistic Liturgy but, in this case, to one way in which the institution narrative itself came to be attached to anaphoral structure.

There is, of course, no question but that Sarapion's epiclesis of the Logos in both the anaphora and the prayer for the sanctification of the baptismal waters (Prayer 7) is the great *crux interpretum* for the document as a whole. While, as noted above, Capelle regarded this as part of Sarapion's own innovative work of substituting the Logos for Holy Spirit, Johannes Betz concluded that:

> The special *Logos-epiclesis* is already well attested for Egypt in Clement, Origen, Athanasius. It must therefore be treated in Sarapion as a primitive formula, not as a correction. If the Prayers of Sarapion do not yet have a fully developed doctrinal precision regarding Logos and

[29]Mazza, "L'anafora di Serapione," 518–19.
[30]Cuming, *Liturgy of St Mark*, 123.

> Pneuma, that is no valid argument against their authenticity.[31]

Betz's conclusion, however, may be stronger than the evidence supplied by Clement,[32] Origen,[33] and Athanasius[34] permits. None of these sources explicitly says that there is a liturgical invocation of the Logos upon the eucharistic gifts or the baptismal waters and it may be that it is only the *content* of Baptism or the Eucharist to which they refer. Nevertheless, Sarapion's explicit epiclesis is certainly consistent with this earlier Alexandrian tradition. Furthermore, it may be significant that in his baptismal catecheses given in Antioch, John Chrysostom refers to the activity of the Logos in the Jordan, saying:

> What happened in the case of our Master's body also happens in the case of your own. Although John appeared to be holding his body by the head, it was the divine Word which led his body down into the streams of Jordan and

[31]Johannes Betz, *Eucharistie in der Schrift und Patristik* (Basel and Vienna: Herder, 1979), 65 n. 8. For other pre-Nicene theological parallels in Justin Martyr and Irenaeus of Lyons, see Santiago Agrelo, "El 'Logos,' potencia divina que hace la eucharistia: Testimonio de san Justino," *Antonianum* 60 (1985): 602–663; and idem, "Epiclesis y eucharistia en S. Ireneo," *Ecclesia Orans* 3 (1986): 7–27.

[32]Clement, *Paedagogus* 1.6.43.2; 2.2.19.4–20.

[33]Origen, *Contra Celsum* 8.33; *In Matt. ser.* 85.

[34]"...καταβαίνει ὁ λόγος εἰς τὸν ἄρτον καὶ τὸ ποτήριον καὶ γίνεται αὐτοῦ σῶμα [*...katabainei ho logos eis ton arton kai to potērion, kai ginetai autou sōma*]" (PG 26:1325).

> baptized him. The Master's body was baptized by the Word, and by the voice of his Father from heaven which said: This is my beloved Son, and by the manifestation of the Holy Spirit which descended upon him. This also happens in the case of your body.[35]

Although this is not a direct reference to an explicit invocation, it is a clear conceptual parallel to the intent of Sarapion's prayer for the sanctification of the baptismal waters (Prayer 7). While absolute proof for the antiquity of a liturgical epiclesis of the Logos is admittedly lacking, it would not be unreasonable to conjecture, therefore, that here, as well, Sarapion is not innovating but merely preserving a traditional theological emphasis and one of its liturgical expressions. And if Betz was correct in his statement that the Logos epiclesis is a "primitive formula," then it well may be the case that the single post-Sanctus epiclesis that some scholars maintain originally existed in Sarapion's anaphora was an epiclesis of the Logos.[36] That the Egyptian anaphoral tradition once contained a

[35]Text in Edward Charles Whitaker, *Documents of the Baptismal Liturgy*, rev. Maxwell E. Johnson (London: SPCK/Collegeville: Pueblo, 2003), 41.

[36]See Anton Baumstark, "Die Anaphora von Thmuis und ihre Überarbeitung durch den hl. Serapion," *Römische Quartalschrift* 18 (1904): 123–42; and Hans Lietzmann, *Mass and Lord's Supper* (Leiden: Brill, 1979). It was Lietzmann's theory that the original shape of the anaphora was an introductory dialogue, preface, Sanctus, and epiclesis, including the entire Sanctus-epiclesis unit, paralleled by the Greek and Coptic versions of St Mark. The (now second)

single short epiclesis, which, through Syrian influence, led to either an elongated one prior to the institution narrative or the addition of a second following that narrative and the anamnesis has been held by scholars for a long time.[37] But another possibility cannot be excluded. It may be that this "Syrian" influence, if it is indeed "Syrian," resulted not in the *addition* of a second epiclesis but in the *division* and *further development* of the *one* native Egyptian epiclesis, which is retained in the early fourth-century anaphoral tradition best represented by the Barcelona Papyrus,[38] together with the Louvain Coptic Fragment,[39] and the Deir Balyzeh Papyrus.[40] But in Sarapion, the British Museum Tablet,[41] and both Greek and Coptic

---

epiclesis of the Logos, according to him, was interpolated as a foreign (Syrian) body into the anaphora.

[37]See René-Georges Coquin, "L'Anaphore alexandrine de saint Marc," *Le Muséon* 82 (1969): 329ff.; Colin H. Roberts and Bernard Capelle, eds, *An Early Euchologium: The Dêr-Balizeh Papyrus* (Louvain: Bureaux du Muséon, 1949), 52; and Joseph Van Haelst, "Une nouvelle reconstitution du papyrus liturgique de Der-Balizeh," *Ephemerides Theologicae Louvanienses* 45 (1969): 210.

[38]See Michael Zheltov, "The Anaphora and the Thanksgiving Prayer from the Barcelona Papyrus: An Underestimated Testimony to the Anaphoral History in the Fourth Century," *Vigiliae Christianae* 62 (2008): 467–504; Nathan Chase, "The Antiochenization of the Egyptian Tradition: An Alternate Approach to the Barcelona Papyrus and Anaphoral Development," *Ecclesia Orans* 34 (2017): 319–67; and idem, "Rethinking Anaphoral Development in Light of the Barcelona Papyrus" (Ph.D. Dissertation, University of Notre Dame, 2020).

[39]PEER4, 99.

[40]PEER4, 100–102

[41]PEER4, 102–104. See also the sixth-century prayer fragment

St Mark there are two epicleses, the first of which still functions partially in its traditional Egyptian post-Sanctus position invoking either God's "power and participation" (Sarapion) or the Holy Spirit upon the sacrifice, but appears to have shifted and probably expanded an explicit consecratory focus to the "Antiochene" position after the institution narrative. Alternatively, of course, in light of the anaphora known as Egyptian Basil,[42] which follows

known as *Vienna Greek papyrus*, which reflects the same feature. In addition to PEER4, 99–100, see Jürgen Hammerstaedt, *Griechische Anaphorenfragmente aus Ägypten und Nubien* (Opladen: Westdeucher Verlag, 1999).

[42]For text see PEER4, 115–23. See also the major study of Gabriele Winkler, *Die Basilius-Anaphora: Edition der beiden armenischen Redaktionen und der relevanten Fragmente, Übersetzung und Zusammenschau aller Versionen im Licht der orientalischen Überlieferungen*, Anaphorae Orientales 2 (Rome: Pontificio Istituto Orientale, 2005); as well as the following, all by the same author: "Nochmals zu den Anfängen der Epiklese und des Sanctus im Eucharistischen Hochgebet," *Theologisches Quartalschrift* 74.3 (1994): 214–31; "Further Observations in Connection with the Early Form of the Epiklesis," *Le Sacrement de l'Initiation: Origines et Prospectives, Patrimoine Syriaque: Actes du colloque III* (Antelias: Centre d'études et de recherches pastorales, 1996), 66–80; and "Weitere Beobachtungen zur frühen Epiklese (den Doxologien und dem Sanctus), Über die Bedeutung der Apokryphen für die Erforschung der Entwicklung der Riten," *Oriens Christianus* 80 (1996): 177–200. See also my summary of this work in Maxwell E. Johnson, "The Origins of the Anaphoral Use of the Sanctus and Epiclesis Revisited: The Contribution of Gabriele Winkler and Its Implications," in H.-J. Feulner, E. Velkovska, and R. Taft, eds, *Crossroad of Cultures*, Orientalia Christiana Analecta 260 (Rome: Pontifical Oriental Institute, 2000), 405–442. See also John R. K. Fenwick, *The Anaphoras of St Basil and St James: An Investigation*

the "Antiochene" structure altogether, it may simply be that Egypt knew more than one way of anaphoral praying and one need not resort to an Antiochene or Syrian hypothesis to account for the location of the second epiclesis.[43] While in Sarapion's text it appears quite possible that an original single post-Sanctus epiclesis has merely been divided and, perhaps, expanded, there is no reason to claim, contra Lietzmann, that the second epiclesis was interpolated as a "foreign body" into the text. That a single epiclesis in Sarapion's anaphora has been divided, for whatever reason, seems quite probable in light of Mary K. Farag's work on δύναμις (*dynamis*) epicleses.[44] That is,

---

into their Common Origin, Orientalia Christiana Analecta 240 (Rome: Pontificio Istituto Orientale, 1992); Anne McGowan, "The Basilian Anaphorae: Rethinking the Question," in Maxwell E. Johnson, ed., *Issues in Eucharistic Praying* (Collegeville, MN: Pueblo, 2010), 219–62; and her *Eucharistic Epicleses, Ancient and Modern: Speaking of the Spirit in the Eucharistic Prayer*, An Alcuin Guide (Collegeville, MN: Pueblo, 2014), 27–86.

[43]See Bryan D. Spinks, "Revisiting Egyptian Anaphoral Development," in David Pitt, Stefanos Alexopoulos, and Christian McConnell, eds, *A Living Tradition: On the Intersection of Liturgical History and Pastoral Practice: Essays in Honor of Maxwell E. Johnson* (Collegeville, MN: Pueblo, 2012); Mary K. Farag, "The Anaphora of St. Thomas the Apostle: Translation and Commentary," *Le Muséon* 123.3 (2010): 317–61; and Nathan P. Chase, "The Antiochenization of the Egyptian Tradition," 319–67.

[44]Mary K. Farag, in "Δύναμις Epicleses: An Athanasian Perspective," *Studia Liturgica* 39 (2009): 63–79. See also the more recent study by Nathan P. Chase, "From *Logos* to Spirit Revisited: The Development of the Epiclesis in Syria and Egypt." *Ecclesia Orans* 39 (2022): 29–63.

while it has often been assumed, including by me, that Sarapion's invocation of God's "power and participation" in the post-Sanctus epiclesis is a reference to the Holy Spirit, Farag demonstrated that such epicleses are designations for the Son and not for the Holy Spirit. Further, she notes that in the second, now consecratory, epiclesis in the anaphora in the British Museum Tablet, both the Holy Spirit and power are invoked upon the Eucharistic gifts. If power designates the Son, then an interesting parallel with Sarapion's Logos epiclesis is certainly suggested, and it would mean that the first epiclesis for "power and participation" is parallel to that of the Logos in the second.

Against Capelle's charge of innovation on the part of Sarapion, the Sanctus unit, bi-partite institution narrative, and the epiclesis of the Logos can certainly be interpreted as the preservation of early euchological forms. This is not to say, however, that they were already present in an earlier stage of the anaphora's development. In fact, if they are omitted as additions to the text, the remainder of the anaphora contains a possible tri-partite form consisting of *praise, offering,* and *supplication,* an anaphoral shape comparable to that of the fragmentary and possibly second-century "anaphora" of the Strasbourg Papyrus.[45] As the following chart

[45]On the question as to whether the Strasbourg papyrus was an anaphora or another type of prayer altogether, see Thomas Talley, "The Literary Structure of the Eucharistic Prayer," *Worship* 58 (1984): 404–20; Kilmartin, "Sacrificium Laudis," 268–87; Geoffrey J. Cuming,

demonstrates, there are significant parallels in Sarapion and Strasbourg that may suggest that some kind of relationship once existed between Sarapion and a Strasbourg type prayer:

Sarapion	Strasbourg
προσηνέγκαμεν ταύτην τὴν ζῶσαν **θυσίαν τὴν** προσφορὰν **τὴν ἀναίμακτον**…	**προσφέρομεν τὴν θυσίαν τὴν** λογικὴν, **τὴν ἀναίμακτον** λατρείαν **ταύτην**…
καὶ **παρακαλοῦμεν** διὰ τῆς **θυσίας ταύτης**… …καὶ ποίησον **μίαν ζῶσαν καθολικὴν ἐκκλησίαν**.	**ἐφηθυσία** καὶ προσφορὰ, δεόμεθα καὶ **παρακαλοῦμεν** σε· μνήσθητι τῆς ἁγίας σου καὶ **μόνης καθολικῆς ἐκκλησίας**…

"The Anaphora of St. Mark: A Study in Development," *Le Muséon* 95 (1982): 115–29; Herman Wegman, "Une anaphore incomplete? Les Fragments sur Papyrus Strasbourg Gr. 254," in R. Van Den Broek and M. J. Vermaseren, eds, *Studies in Gnosticism and Hellenistic Religions* (Leiden: Brill, 1981), 42–50; Bryan D. Spinks, "A Complete Anaphora? A Note on Strasbourg Gr. 254," *The Heythrop Journal* 25 (1984): 51–59, and Michael Zheltov, "The Anaphora and the Thanksgiving Prayer from the Barcelona Papyrus: An Underestimated Testimony to the Anaphoral History in the Fourth Century," *Vigiliae Christianae* 62 (2008): 467–504. While, with the exception of Spinks and Zheltov, most liturgical scholars today accept that the Strasbourg Papyrus was itself a complete anaphora, it is of little consequence here since something like it certainly served as a source not only for Sarapion's anaphora but also for the anaphora in *Mystagogical Catechesis* 5, attributed to Cyril of Jerusalem (see St Cyril of Jerusalem, *Lectures on the Christian Sacraments: The Procatechesis and the Five Mystagogical Catecheses ascribed to St Cyril of Jerusalem*, ed. and trans. Maxwell E. Johnson, Popular Patristics Series 57 [Yonkers, NY: St Vladimir's Seminary Press, 2017]) and, of course, both the Coptic and Greek versions of St Mark (see Cuming, *Liturgy of St. Mark*, 155–56).

Sarapion (*continued*)	Strasbourg (*continued*)
Σὲ γὰρ τὸν ἀγένητον **ἐπεκαλεσάμεθα…**	δι' πάντας τοὺς **ἐπικαλουμένους** τὸ ὄνομα σου…
Παρακαλοῦμεν δὲ καὶ ὑπὲρ πάντων **τῶν κεκοιμημένων,** ὧν ἐστιν καὶ ἡ ἀνάμνησις· μετὰ τὴν ὑποβολὴν τῶν ὀνομάτων ἁγίασον **τὰς ψυχὰς** ταύτας, σὺ γὰρ πάσας γινώσκεις· ἁγίασον πάσας τὰς ἐν κυρίῳ **κοιμηθείσας…**	**τῶν κεκοιμημένων τὰς ψυχὰς** ἀνάπαυσον. Μνήσθητι τῶν ἐπὶ τῆς σήμερον ἡμέρας τὴν ὑπόμνησιν ποιούμεθα· καὶ ὧν λέγομεν καὶ ὧν οὐ λέγομεν **ὀνόματα.**
prosēnenkamen tautēn tēn *zōsan…* ***thysian tēn*** *prosphoran tēn* ***anaimakton…*** *kai* ***parakaloumen*** *dia tēs* ***thysias*** *tautēs…* *…kai poēson* ***mian zōsan katholikēn ekklēsian.***	***prospheromen tēn thysian tēn*** *logikēn, tēn* ***anaimakton*** *latreian* ***tautēn…*** ***ephēthysia*** *kai prosphora, deometha kai* ***parakaloumen*** *se: mnēsthēti tēs hagias sou kai* ***monēs katholikēs ekklēsias…***
Se gar ton agenēton ***epekalesametha…***	*di' pantas tous* ***epikaloumenous*** *to onoma sou…*
Parakaloumen de kai hyper pantōn ***tōn kekoimēmenōn,*** *hōn estin kai hē anamnesis. meta tēn hypobolēn tōn* ***onomatōn;*** *hagiason* ***tas psychas*** *tautas, sy gar pasas ginōskeis; hagiason pasas tas en kyriō* ***koimētheisas…***	***tōn kekoimēmenōn tas psychas*** *anapauson. Mnysthēti tōn epi tēs sēmeron hēmeras tēn hypomnēsin poioumetha kai hōn legomen kai hōn ou legomen* ***onomata***

Whatever the specific relationship may be to the prayer of the Strasbourg Papyrus, both the overall structure and even literary parallels suggest that what the "author" of the anaphora did was to take a Strasbourg-type prayer, whether eucharistic or not, and add, in piece-meal fashion, the remainder of the prayer in the following manner:

(1) The first thing to be added was probably the Alexandrian Sanctus unit with its epiclesis, a unit that, if Kretschmar, Taft, and I are correct, was already present in late third-century Alexandria. Along with its four concomitant introductory petitions for the fruits of Communion, this entire unit was not added to the conclusion of this Strasbourg-type prayer but interpolated into the middle of it, after praise, at the very place where offering and intercession occurred.

(2) The traditional Egyptian focus on this offering as taking place within the "preface" was too strong, however, to be merely transformed or omitted. So, following the post-Sanctus epiclesis, both the offering and its related intercessions—διὰ τῆς (*dia tēs*)—were retained. But the tense of the offering verb was now changed from present (προσφέρομεν, *prospheromen*) to aorist (προσηνέγκαμεν, *prosēnenkamen*) in order to

underscore the fact that this sacrifice had already taken place.[46]

(3) Then, perhaps under Syrian influence, but inspired by a source common to *Apostolic Constitutions* 7.25 and Sarapion, the unique bi-partite institution narrative was added between offering and intercessions.

(4) Next, under possible Syrian influence, the one post-Sanctus epiclesis was expanded and divided with its specific consecratory focus and prayer for the fruits of Communion shifted to the "Antiochene" or Basilian location after the institution narrative.

(5) Finally, the intercessions or prayers for the fruits of Communion, displaced from the "preface" and continuing their anaphoral descent, arrived at the end of the prayer, also in the "Antiochene" or Basilian position.[47]

However, because these additions to the prayer appear to reflect early forms or archaic orientations themselves, there is no compelling reason why the

[46]Alphonse Raes once called the tense of the post-Sanctus or post-anamnesis offering verb in a variety of Egyptian anaphoras, including even in Egyptian Basil, the "famous aorist." See Alphonse Raes, "Un nouveau document de la Liturgie de S. Basile," *Orientalia Christiana Periodica* 26 (1960): 401–10.

[47]On this, see Nathan P. Chase, "The Fruits of Communion in the Classical Anaphoras," *Orientalia Christiana Periodica* 87 (2021): 5–70, esp. 21–24 and 37–41.

entire anaphora should not be dated any later than the middle of the fourth century. *Pace* both Capelle and Botte, therefore, Sarapion's anaphora remains a potentially reliable fourth-century witness that preserves a number of important elements characteristic of earlier euchological traditions.

iv. Theological Analysis

Cuming's response to Botte's contention that the document represented a later deliberate Pneumatomachian attempt to "put the Holy Spirit in the shade" has already been noted. That Cuming was correct in pointing to the close relationship between Logos and Spirit in Athanasius may be taken as confirmed by the work of Charles Kannengiesser on Athanasius' theology of the Spirit between Nicea and Constantinople.[1] Kannengiesser, however, pointed to the works of Athanasius prior to his *Epistulae ad Serapionem* and noted that in his *Orationes contra Arianos I–II* (339–40) the Spirit is regarded as the perfect gift of the Son who sanctifies, the "power" (δύναμις, *dynamis*) of the Son in whom and through whom the Son acts, and as the one who acts and dwells in us.

> The Spirit which *dwells* among us becomes our *relative,* he is *participated in* by "us" *(meteschomen . . .)* by the same title and by the same grace as the Incarnate Logos is working salvation in us, the Spirit *speaks to us,* as once to the prophets, but he never speaks of himself: it *is* the Word who gives to the Spirit to speak, who makes the "seal" eloquent, the "gift" intelligible.[2]

[1]Charles Kannengiesser, "Athanasius of Alexandria and the Holy Spirit between Nicea I and Constantinople I," *The Irish Theological Quarterly* 48 (1981): 166–79.

[2]Kannengiesser, "Athanasius of Alexandria and the Holy Spirit," 176.

Bearing in mind Farag's above-noted critique of δύναμις (*dynamis*) as a reference not to the Spirit but to the Son, Kannengiesser's Athanasian understanding of the close working of the Logos and the Holy Spirit lends credibility to Cuming's defense of Sarapion's orthodoxy, and, hence, to a traditional dating for the text.

Even more, however, can certainly be said here in response to Botte's thesis. Without any knowledge of Botte's position on Sarapion's heterodoxy, it is interesting that in her work on trinitiarian theology, Catherine Mowry LaCugna pointed precisely to the juxtaposition of "Father" with "Only-begotten" in Sarapion's prayers, noting that this is an indication of an anti-Arian orientation. She writes:

> In the *Euchologion* of Serapion, a mid-fourth-century Egyptian liturgy, the God addressed in prayer is now often named "Father of the Only-Begotten Son"...The substitution of "Son" for "Christ" highlights the divinity of Christ, and conveys that the mediation of our prayer takes place through Christ in both his humankind *and* divinity....With...the increasingly common reference to Christ as the only-begotten, the name of God as Father also takes on a more pronounced intratrinitarian meaning. This is in keeping with concurrent doctrinal developments.... Prior to the fourth century, in the Bible

> and early creeds and in Greek theology, Father was a synonym for God and did not denote God's special eternal relationship as Begetter of the Son.[3]

Botte's suggestion, therefore, that the use of ἀγένητος (*agenētos*) in juxtaposition to μονογενοῦς (*monogenous*) was a sign of an Arian or semi-Arian theological orientation is simply not supported by the document. With the frequent use of "Father" and "Only-begotten" there is nothing in Sarapion's text to suggest that he understands the Son as "originated" or "made," or in any way different from what is suggested by Athanasius above.

Further, in his classic study of the theology and spirituality of the eucharistic prayer, Louis Bouyer drew attention to the four references to the Holy Spirit in the "preface" of Sarapion's anaphora: "Give us [the] Spirit of light, in order that we may know You the true (God) and Jesus Christ whom You sent. Give us [the] Holy Spirit, in order that we may be able to proclaim and describe Your inexpressible mysteries. Let the Lord Jesus speak in us and let [the] Holy Spirit also hymn You through us ..." And with regard to this he wrote: "We cannot understand how a *pneumatomachos* could have introduced the Spirit in a number of places where he does

[3]Catherine Mowry LaCugna, *God for Us: The Trinity and Christian Life* (San Francisco: Harper Collins, 1991), 116.

not figure in any other eucharistic liturgy."[4] Beyond this, four other points may be made.

First of all, while Botte pointed to the presence of ὑπόστασις (*hypostasis*), rather than φύσις or κτίσις (*physis, ktisis*), in juxtaposition to ἀγένητος (*agenētos*) in the anaphoral preface, he did not note that in the very next phrase φύσις (*physis*) actually appears (τὸν δι' αὐτοῦ λαληθέντα καὶ ἑρμηνευθέντα καὶ γνωσθέντα τῇ γενητῇ φύσει, *ton di' autou lalēthenta kai hermēneuthenta kai gnōsthenta tē genētē* physei).

Second, a simple word count reveals that the "astonishing frequency" of ἀγένητος (*agenētos*) is actually only nine occurrences in the entire document. And, of these nine, three appear within the anaphora itself with the other six occurring only in Prayers 6, 7, 13, 26, 27, and 28, all of which, it has been suggested above, appear to belong to the same literary stratum of the text.

Third, Botte's statement that Holy Spirit "always" occurs without the definite article in the text except for Prayer 16 is simply incorrect. In the concluding doxology of Prayer 8 τῷ ἁγίῳ πνεύματι (*to hagio pneumati*) appears and τὸ ἅγιόν σου πνεῦμα (*to hagion sou pneuma*) occurs in Prayer 10. In Prayer 11, even if "holy" is not present here, it is "*the* Spirit of the Only-begotten" who is invoked on the candidate for the presbyteral office. And Prayer 15 asks that those who are being baptized may be "renewed in *the* Spirit" (καὶ τῷ πνεύματι ἀνανεωθέντες, *kai tō pneumati ananeōthentes*).

[4]Bouyer, *Eucharist*, 207 n. 20.

Fourth and finally, Botte asked whether the uncoordinate form of the doxology could be considered "orthodox" still in 350–60. Not only is it significant that there is an occurrence of the definite article with the Holy Spirit in one of Sarapion's concluding doxologies, but, based on the following doxological citations in contemporary writings of Athanasius, the answer to his question is *yes*:

> *Ad episcopos Aegypti* 23 (356): *through* whom *to* the Father be glory and dominion *in* the Holy Spirit, both now and forever, world without end. Amen. (NPNF[2] 4:235)

> *Apologia de fuga* 27 (357): *in* Christ Jesus our Lord, *through* whom *to* the Father *in* the Holy Spirit be glory and power forever and ever. Amen. (NPNF[2] 4:265)

Similarly, it is well known that even for Basil of Caesarea—writing *De Spiritu Sancto* in defense of the coordinate form of the doxology against his Pneumatomachian critics in 375—the uncoordinate form was still considered to be "orthodox":

> *De Spiritu Sancto* 1.3: Lately when I pray with the people, some of those present observed that I render the glory due to God in both ways, namely, to the Father, with the Son together

> with the Holy Spirit, and to the Father, through the Son, in the Holy Spirit.[5]
>
> *De Spiritu Sancto* 25.59: We have used both expressions because we have found that the faithful use both. We believe that glory is similarly rendered to the Spirit by each expression … (PPS 42:96)
>
> *De Spiritu Sancto* 26.63: The doxology that we offer in the Spirit does not confess the dignity of the Spirit, but rather confesses our weakness. We thus indicate that we are not sufficient to glorify [God] from ourselves; rather, our sufficiency is in the Holy Spirit … (PPS 42:102)

In all cases, therefore, the thesis of Botte that the text of Sarapion represents a conscious heretical theological position stemming from a time later than the middle of the fourth century may be rejected as lacking any firm foundation. It is refuted, in fact, by such "orthodox" theologians as Athanasius of Alexandria and Basil of Caesarea themselves.[6]

[5]St Basil the Great, *On the Holy Spirit*, trans. Stephen Hildebrand, Popular Patristics Series 42 (Yonkers, NY: St Vladimir's Seminary Press, 2011), 29.

[6]See the work of Mihálykó, *The Christian Liturgical Papyri*, 229–30, and 230 n. 6 in support of this position.

v. Conclusion

On literary, liturgical, and theological grounds, there is no basis for accepting the theses of either Capelle or Botte. Against Capelle, the document appears to be a collection of diverse prayers reflecting different liturgical strata and is not a homogenous literary piece written by a single author from a particular theological stance, *avant-garde* or otherwise. Rather, Sarapion's prayers represent *preservation,* not innovation. Against Botte, the theology of the document is orthodox, in its mid-fourth century theology, or at least consistent with other orthodox figures of the same historical period. Without Botte's thesis, a thesis accepted in the past by others without further qualification or research, so much so that it was common to refer to Sarapion as "Pseudo-Sarapion," there is no reason to doubt the traditional scholarly view of the liturgical importance and traditional mid-fourth-century date of this document, a view emphasized both by Cuming and me among contemporary scholars. And today it is easily asserted that the current scholarly consensus, in spite of disputes over various details here and there, is that the name of Sarapion of Thmuis, perhaps as editor if not author, should remain, in the words of Brightman, "as a symbol of the date and provenance of the prayers"—that is, mid-fourth century Egypt at the latest.[1]

[1] Brightman, "The Sacramentary of Serapion," 91.

vi. Select Bibliography

A. Texts and Editions

1. Manuscript

MS Lavra 149 (housed in the Library of the Great Lavra Monastery on Mount Athos, Greece)

2. Editions

Brightman, Frank Edward. "The Sacramentary of Serapion," *Journal of Theological Studies* 1 (1900): 88–113, 247–277.

Dimitrievskij, A., *Ein Euchologium aus dem 4. Jahrhundert, verfasst von Sarapion, Bischoff von Thmuis*. Kiev, 1894.

Funk, Francis Xavier. *Didascalia et Constitutiones Apostolorum*, volume 2. Paderborn: Ferdinand Schoeningh, 1905.

Johnson, Maxwell E. *The Prayers of Sarapion of Thmuis: A Literary, Liturgical, and Theological Analysis.* Orientalia Christiana Analecta 249. Rome: Pontifical Oriental Institute, 1995.

Wobbermin, Georg. *Altchristliche liturgische Stücke aus der Kirche Ägyptens nebst einem dogmatischen Brief des Bischofs Serapion von Thmuis.* Texte und Untersuchungen zur Geschichte der altchristlichen Literatur 17, 3. Leipzig and Berlin: J. C. Hinrichs, 1898.

B. Translations

Barrett-Leonard, R. J. S., *The Sacramentary of Sarapion of Thmuis: A Text for Students, with Introduction, Translation, and Commentary*. Alcuin/GROW Liturgical Study 25. Bramcote/Nottingham: Grove Books, Ltd., 1993.

Deiss, Lucien. *Springtime of the Liturgy*. Translated by Matthew J. O'Connell. Collegeville, MN: The Liturgical Press, 1979, repr. 1991.[2]

Hamman, André. *Early Christian Prayers*. Translated by Walter Mitchell. Chicago: Henry Regnery Co., 1961.[3]

Johnson, Maxwell E. *The Prayers of Sarapion of Thmuis: A Literary, Liturgical, and Theological Analysis*. Orientalia Christiana Analecta 249. Rome: Pontifical Oriental Institute, 1995.

Wordsworth, John. *Bishop Sarapion's Prayer Book: An Egyptian Pontifical Dated Probably About A.D. 350–356*. London: Society for Promoting Christian Knowledge, 1899; 2nd ed. 1923; repr. Hamden, CT: Archon Books, 1964.

[2]All prayers are based on the French of Deiss' work, not directly on the Greek text.

[3]All prayers are based on the French of Hamman's work, not directly on the Greek text.

C. Studies

Botte, Bernard. "L'Eucologe de Sérapion est-il authentique?" *Oriens Christianus* 48 (1964): 50–56.

Capelle, Bernard. "L' Anaphore de Sérapion. Essai d'exégèse." *Le Muséon* 59 (1946): 425–43 = *Travaux liturgiques de doctrine et d'histoire*, volume 2. Louvain: Abbaye du Mont-César, 1962. Pages 344–58.

Cuming, Geoffrey. "Thmuis Revisited: Another Look at the Prayers of Bishop Sarapion." *Theological Studies* 41 (1980): 568–75.

Dix, Gregory. "Primitive Consecration Prayers." *Theology* 37 (1938): 261–83.

Johnson, Maxwell E. "The Archaic Nature of the Sanctus, Institution Narrative, and Epiclesis of the Logos in the Anaphora Ascribed to Sarapion of Thmuis." In Robert Taft, editor. *The Christian East, Its Institutions & Its Thought: A Critical Reflection: Papers of the International Scholarly Congress for the 75th Anniversary of the Pontifical Oriental Institute Rome, 30 May–5 June 1993*. Orientalia Christiana Analecta 250. Rome: Pontifical Oriental Institute, 1996. Pages 671–702.

Johnson, Maxwell E. "The Baptismal Rite and Anaphora in the Prayers of Sarapion of Thmuis: An Assessment of a Recent 'Judicious Reassessment.'" *Worship* 73.2 (March 1999): 140–68.

Johnson, Maxwell E. *The Prayers of Sarapion of Thmuis: A Literary, Liturgical, and Theological*

Analysis. Orientalia Christiana Analecta 249. Rome: Pontifical Oriental Institute, 1995.

Rodopoulos, Panteleimon E. "The Sacrament of Serapion." *θεολογία* 28 (1957): 252–75, 420–39, 578–91; 29 (1958): 45–54, 208–217.

Spinks, Bryan D. "The Integrity of the Anaphora of Sarapion of Thmuis and Liturgical Methodology." *Journal of Theological Studies* 49.1 (1998): 136–44.

Spinks, Bryan D. "Sarapion of Thmuis and Baptismal Practice in Early Christian Egypt: The Need for a Judicious Reassessment." *Worship* 72 (May, 1998): 255–70.

Taft, Robert. "The Interpolation of the Sanctus into the Anaphora: When and Where? A Review of the Dossier: Part I." *Orientalia Christiana Periodica* 57 (1991): 281–308.

Taft, Robert. "The Interpolation of the Sanctus into the Anaphora: When and Where? A Review of the Dossier: Part II." *Orientalia Christiana Periodica* 58 (1992): 83–121.

Taft, Robert. *The Liturgy of the Hours in East and West.* Collegeville, MN: The Liturgical Press, 1986.

The Prayers of SAINT SARAPION The Bishop of Thmuis

Text and Translation

The Greek text and English translation of the Prayers in MS Lavra 149 is a corrected version of my 1995 edition, *The Prayers of Sarapion of Thmuis: A Literary, Liturgical, and Theological Analysis*, with the editions of Wobbermin, Brightman, and Funk used for comparative purposes. While the texts of Brightman and Funk are generally found to be in close agreement with this manuscript, references to variant readings in all four documents and to other textual notes in the following are made by lower case letters (a, b, c, etc.) superscripted in the text and listed at the end of each prayer or section of a prayer. The documents themselves are referred to according to the following sigla:

> A = MS Lavra 149, B = Brightman, F = Funk, and W = Wobbermin.

Biblical citations and allusions appear as notes in the margin outside the Greek text. While Wobbermin provided only a few references to biblical texts, Brightman offered many, which were simply copied by Funk, who placed them within quotation marks in the text. A large number of these remain in the following text, along with others that have not been previously noted, but only those words and phrases that are taken directly from or seem to be suggested by biblical passages are included. However, because it is often difficult to tell whether certain words and phrases are actually intended to be biblical allusions or are merely part of the Church's general liturgical and theological vocabulary, it is impossible to be completely accurate. References to the Old Testament are made according to the titles and numbering system of the Septuagint.

[1] Εὐχὴ Προσφόρου Σαραπίωνος ἐπισκόπου

Ἄξιον καὶ δίκαιόν ἐστιν σὲ τὸν ἀγένητον πατέρα τοῦ μονογενοῦς Ἰησοῦ Χριστοῦ αἰνεῖν ὑμνεῖν δοξολογεῖν. Αἰνοῦμεν σὲ ἀγένητε Θεὲ ἀνεξιχνίαστε ἀνέκφραστε ἀκατανόητε πάσῃ γενητῇ ὑποστάσει. Αἰνοῦμεν σὲ τὸν γιγνωσκόμενον ὑπὸ τοῦ υἱοῦ τοῦ μονογενοῦς, τὸν δι᾽ αὐτοῦ λαληθέντα καὶ ἑρμηνευθέντα καὶ γνωσθέντα τῇ γενητῇ φύσει. Αἰνοῦμεν σὲ τὸν γιγνώσκοντα τὸν υἱὸν καὶ ἀποκαλύπτοντα τοῖς ἁγίοις τὰς περὶ αὐτοῦ δόξας· τὸν γιγνωσκόμενον ὑπὸ τοῦ γεγεννημένου σου λόγου καὶ ὁρμώμενον καὶ διερμηνευόμενον τοῖς ἁγίοις. Αἰνοῦμεν σὲ πάτερ ἀόρατε, χορηγὲ τῆς ἀθανασίας. σὺ εἶ ἡ πηγὴ τῆς ζωῆς, ἡ πηγὴ τοῦ φωτός, ἡ πηγὴ πάσης χάριτος καὶ πάσης ἀληθείας, φιλάνθρωπε καὶ φιλόπτωχε, ὁ πᾶσιν καταλλασσόμενος καὶ πάντας πρὸς ἑαυτὸν διὰ τῆς ἐπιδημίας τοῦ ἀγαπήτου σου υἱοῦ ἕλκων. δεόμεθα ποίησον ἡμᾶς ζῶντας ἀνθρώπους· δὸς ἡμῖν πνεῦμα φωτός, ἵνα γνῶμεν σὲ τὸν ἀληθινὸν καὶ ὅν ἀπέστειλας Ἰησοῦν Χριστόν· δὸς ἡμῖν πνεῦμα ἅγιον, ἵνα δυνηθῶμεν ἐξειπεῖν καὶ διηγήσασθαι τὰ ἄρρητά σου μυστήρια. λαλησάτω ἐν ἡμῖν ὁ κύριος Ἰησοῦς καὶ ἅγιον πνεῦμα καὶ ὑμνησάτω σὲ δι᾽ ἡμῶν.

Σὺ γὰρ ὅ ὑπεράνω πάσης ἀρχῆς καὶ ἐξουσίας καὶ δυ[νά]μεως καὶ κυριότητος καὶ παντὸς ὀνόματος ὀνομαζομένου οὐ μόνον ἐν τῷ αἰῶνι τούτῳ ἀλλὰ καὶ ἐν τῷ μέλλοντι· σοὶ παραστήκουσις χίλιαι χιλιάδες καὶ μύριαι

Mt 11.27 · Col 1.26–27 · Jn 1.4, 14; 8.12 · 2 Cor 5.19 · Jn 17.3 · 1 Cor 14.2; Col 4.3 · 1 Cor 14.2; Col 4.3

1 Σαραπίονος A | 10 γεγεγημένου A | 26 παραστήσουσι A

[1] Prayer of Offering of Bishop Sarapion

It is right and just to praise You, to hymn You, to glorify You, the uncreated Father of the Only-begotten Jesus Christ. We praise You, uncreated God, incomprehensible, inexpressible, inconceivable to every created substance. We praise You who are known by the Only-begotten Son, You who through Him were spoken and interpreted and made known to created nature. We praise You who know the Son and who reveal to the saints the glories concerning Him; You who are known by Your begotten Word and known and interpreted to the saints. We praise You, invisible Father, provider of immortality. You are the source of life, the source of light, the source of all grace and truth. Lover of humankind and lover of the poor, You are reconciled to all and draw all to Yourself through the coming of Your beloved Son. We pray, make us living people. Give us [the] Spirit of light, in order that we may know You the true [God] and Jesus Christ whom You sent. Give us [the] Holy Spirit, in order that we may be able to proclaim and describe Your inexpressible mysteries. Let the Lord Jesus speak in us and let [the] Holy Spirit also hymn You through us.[1]

For You are above all rule and authority and power and dominion and every name being named, not only in this age but also in the coming one. Beside You stand a thousand thousands and a myriad myriads of angels,

[1] Although ὑμνησάτω is a singular third-person imperative and calls for a singular subject, the sense of this phrase seems to be "Let the Lord Jesus and Holy Spirit speak in us and hymn You through us."

μυριάδες ἀγγέλων ἀρχαγγέλων θρόνων κυριοτήτων ἀρχῶν ἐξουσιῶν σοὶ παραστήκουσιν τὰ δύο τιμιώτατα σεραφεὶμ ἑξαπτέρυγα, δυσὶν μὲν πτέρυξιν καλύπτοντα τὸ πρόσωπον, δυσὶ δὲ τοὺς πόδας, δυσὶ δὲ πετόμενα, καὶ ἁγιάζοντα· μεθ' ὧν δέξαι καὶ τὸν ἡμέτερον ἁγιασμὸν λεγόντων Ἅγιος ἅγιος ἅγιος κύριος σαβαώθ πλήρης ὁ οὐρανὸς καὶ ἡ γῆ τῆς δόξης σου. Πλήρης ἐστὶν ὁ οὐρανός, πλήρης ἐστὶν καὶ ἡ γῆ τῆς μεγαλοπρεποῦς σου δόξης κύριε τῶν δυνάμεων πλήρωσον καὶ τὴν θυσίαν ταύτην τῆς σῆς δυνάμεως καὶ τῆς σῆς μεταλήψεως· σοὶ γὰρ προσηνέγκαμεν ταύτην τὴν ζῶσαν θυσίαν τὴν προσφορὰν τὴν ἀναίμακτον.

Σοὶ προσηνέγκαμεν τὸν ἄρτον τοῦτον, τὸ ὁμοίωμα τοῦ σώματος τοῦ μονογενούς. ὁ ἄρτος οὗτος του ἁγίου σώματός ἐστιν ὁμοίωμα, ὅτι ὁ κύριος Ἰησοῦς Χριστὸς ἐν ᾗ νυκτὶ παρεδίδοτο ἔλαβεν ἄρτον καὶ ἔκλασεν καὶ ἐδίδου τοῖς μαθηταῖς ἑαυτοῦ λέγων λάβετε καὶ φάγετε, τοῦτό ἐστιν τὸ σῶμά μου τὸ ὑπὲρ ὑμῶν κλώμενον εἰς ἄφεσιν ἁμαρτιῶν. διὰ τοῦτο καὶ ἡμεῖς τὸ ὁμοίωμα τοῦ θανάτου ποιοῦντες τὸν ἄρτον προσηνέγκαμεν, καὶ παρακαλοῦμεν διὰ τῆς θυσίας ταύτης καταλλάγηθι πᾶσιν ἡμῖν καὶ ἱλάσθητι Θεὲ τῆς ἀληθείας· καὶ ὥσπερ ὁ ἄρτος οὗτος ἐσκορπισμένος ἦν ἐπάνω τῶν ὀρέων καὶ συναχθεὶς ἐγένετο εἰς ἕν, οὕτω καὶ τὴν ἁγίαν σου ἐκκλησίαν σύναξον ἐκ παντὸς ἔθνους καὶ πάσης χώρας καὶ πάσης πόλεως καὶ κώμης καὶ οἴκου καὶ ποίησον μίαν ζῶσαν καθολικὴν ἐκκλησίαν. Προσηνέγκαμεν δὲ καὶ τὸ ποτήριον τὸ

Dan 7.10 | Col 1.16 | Is 6.2–3 | Is 6.3 | Ps 83.1 | Rom 12.1 | 1 Cor 11.23–24; Mt 26.26; Mk 14.22; Lk 22.19| Rom 6.5; 1 Cor 11.26|Ps 30.6 | *Didache* 9.4.

5 πετώμενα A | 5 δέξε A | 22 τοῦτος A

archangels, thrones, dominions, principalities, and powers. Beside You stand the two most-honored, six-winged seraphim. With two wings they cover the face, and with two the feet, and with two they fly, sanctifying. With them receive also our sanctification as we say: Holy, holy, holy Lord of Sabaoth; heaven and earth are full of Your glory. Full is heaven and full also is the earth of Your majestic glory, Lord of powers. Fill also this sacrifice with Your power and with Your participation. For to You we offered this living sacrifice, the unbloody offering.

To You we offered this bread, the likeness of the Body of the Only-begotten. This bread is the likeness of the holy Body. For the Lord Jesus Christ, in the night when was betrayed, took bread, broke it, and gave it to His disciples, saying: "Take and eat, this is My Body which is broken for you for the forgiveness of sins." Therefore, we also offered the bread making the likeness of the death. And we implore You through this sacrifice, God of truth: be reconciled to us all and be merciful. And as this bread was scattered over the mountains and, when gathered together, became one, so also gather Your holy Church out of every nation and every region and every city and village and house, and make one living catholic Church. And we also offered the cup, the likeness of the Blood. For the Lord Jesus Christ, taking a cup after supper, said to the disciples: "Take, drink, this is the New Covenant, which is My Blood poured out for you for the forgiveness of sins." Therefore, we also offered the cup presenting the likeness of Blood. God of truth, let Your holy Word come to dwell upon this bread in order that the

1 Cor 11.25; Mt 26.27–28; Mk 14.23–24; Lk 22.20 | Ps 30.6

ὁμοίωμα τοῦ αἵματος, ὅτι κύριος Ἰησοῦς Χριστὸς λαβὼν ποτήριον μετὰ τὸ δειπνῆσαι ἔλεγεν τοῖς ἑαυτοῦ μαθηταῖς· λάβετε πίετε, τοῦτό ἐστιν ἡ καινὴ διαθήκη, ὅ ἐστιν τὸ αἷμα μου τὸ ὑπὲρ ὑμῶν ἐκχυνόμενον εἰς ἄφεσιν ἁμαρτημάτων. διὰ τοῦτο προσηνέγκαμεν καὶ ἡμεῖς τὸ ποτήριον ὁμοίωμα αἵματος προσάγοντες. Ἐπιδημησάτω θεὲ τῆς ἀληθείας ὁ ἅγιός σου λόγος ἐπὶ τὸν ἄρτον τοῦτον, ἵνα γένηται ὁ ἄρτος σῶμα τοῦ λόγου, καὶ ἐπὶ τὸ ποτήριον τοῦτο, ἵνα γένηται τὸ ποτήριον αἷμα τῆς ἀληθείας.

1 Cor 11.34| Ps 30.6

καὶ ποίησον πάντας τοὺς κοινωνοῦντας φάρμακον ζωῆς λαβεῖν εἰς θεραπείαν παντὸς νοσήματος καὶ εἰς ἐνδυνάμωσιν πάσης προκοπῆς καὶ ἀρετῆς, μὴ εἰς κατάκρισιν θεὲ τῆς ἀληθείας μηδὲ εἰς ἔλεγχον καὶ ὄνειδος. Σὲ γὰρ τὸν ἀγένητον ἐπεκαλεσάμεθα διὰ τοῦ μονογενοῦς ἐν ἁγίῳ πνεύματι ἐλεηθήτω ὁ λαὸς οὗτος, προκοπῆς ἀξιωθήτω, ἀποσταλήτωσαν ἄγγελοι συμπαρόντες τῷ λαῷ εἰς κατάργησιν τοῦ πονηροῦ καὶ εἰς βεβαίωσιν τῆς ἐκκλησίας. Παρακαλοῦμεν δὲ καὶ ὑπὲρ πάντων τῶν κεκοιμημένων, ὧν ἐστιν καὶ ἡ ἀνάμνησις.

μετὰ τὴν ὑποβολὴν τῶν ὀνομάτων

1 Cor 15.18; Rev 14.13 | Jn 14.2

ἁγίασον τὰς ψυχὰς ταύτας, σὺ γὰρ πάσας γινώσκεις· ἁγίασον πάσας τὰς ἐν κυρίῳ κοιμηθείσας καὶ συγκαταρίθμησον πάσαις ταῖς ἁγίαις σου δυνάμεσιν καὶ δὸς αὐτοῖς τόπον καὶ μονὴν ἐν τῇ βασιλείᾳ σου. Δέξαι δὲ καὶ τὴν εὐχαριστίαν τοῦ λαοῦ καὶ εὐλόγησον τοὺς

17 κατήργησιν A | 20 This "rubric" is not separated from the body of the prayer in A, W, or F. | 24 δέξε A

bread may become the Body of the Word, and upon this cup in order that the cup may become the Blood of truth.

And make all those who commune to receive a medicine of life for the healing of every illness, and for the strengthening of every advancement and virtue, not for condemnation, God of truth, nor for testing and reproach. For we called upon You, the Uncreated, through the Only-begotten in [the] Holy Spirit. Let this people receive mercy. Let them be made worthy of advancement. Let angels be present with them for abolishing evil and for establishing the Church. And we call out also for all who have fallen asleep, for whom also the memorial [is made].

After the Announcement of the Names

Sanctify these souls for You know them all. Sanctify all who have fallen asleep in the Lord. Number them with all Your holy powers, and give them a place and a mansion in Your kingdom. And receive also the thanksgiving of the people and bless those who offer their offerings and thanksgiving [prayers]. Give to this entire people health, wholeness, cheerfulness, and every advancement of soul

προσενεγκόντας τὰ πρόσφορα καὶ τὰς εὐχαριστίας καὶ χάρισαι ὑγείαν καὶ ὁλοκληρίαν καὶ εὐθυμίαν καὶ πᾶσαν προκοπὴν ψυχῆς καὶ σώματος ὅλῳ τῷ λαῷ τούτῳ· διὰ τοῦ μονογενοῦς σου Ἰησοῦ Χριστοῦ ἐν ἁγίῳ πνεύματι. Ὥσπερ ἦν καὶ ἐστὶν καὶ ἔσται εἰς γενεὰς γενεῶν καὶ εἰς τοὺς σύμπαντας αἰῶνας τῶν αἰώνων. ἀμήν.

[2] μετὰ τὴν εὐχὴν ἡ κλάσις καὶ ἐν τῇ κλάσει εὐχή

Καταξίωσον ἡμᾶς τῆς κοινωνίας καὶ ταύτης θεὲ τῆς ἀλη-
Ps 30.6 θείας καὶ ποίησον τὰ σώματα ἡμῶν χωρῆσαι ἁγνείαν καὶ τὰς ψυχὰς φρόνησιν καὶ γνῶσιν καὶ σόφισον ἡμάς θεὲ τῶν οἰκτιρμῶν διὰ τῆς μεταλήψεως τοῦ σώματος καὶ τοῦ αἵματος· ὅτι διὰ τοῦ μονογενοῦς σοὶ ἡ δόξα καὶ τὸ κράτος ἐν ἁγίῳ πνεύματι καὶ νῦν καὶ εἰς τοὺς σύμπαντας αἰῶνας τῶν αἰώνων. ἀμήν.

[3] Μετὰ τὸ διαδοῦναι τὴν κλάσιν τοῖς κληρικοῖς χειροθεσία λαοῦ

Ἐκτείνω τὴν χεῖρα ἐπὶ τὸν λαὸν τοῦτον καὶ δέομαι ἐκταθῆναι τὴν τῆς ἀληθείας χεῖρα καὶ δοθῆναι εὐλογίαν τῷ λαῷ τούτῳ διὰ τὴν σὴν φιλανθρωπίαν θεὲ τῶν οἰκτιρμῶν καὶ τὰ μυστήρια τὰ παρόντα· χεὶρ εὐλαβείας καὶ δυνάμεως καὶ σωφρονισμοῦ καὶ καθαρότητος καὶ πάσης ὁσιότητος εὐλογησάτω τὸν λαὸν τοῦτον καὶ διατηρησάτω εἰς προκοπὴν καὶ βελτίωσιν· διὰ τοῦ μονογενοῦς

2 ὑγείαι A | 7 εὐχήν L | 9 ἁγνίαν L | 13 καὶ omitted by W | 15 διαδόναι W

and body. Through Your Only-begotten Jesus Christ in [the] Holy Spirit. As it was and is and will be to generations of generations and to all the ages of ages. Amen.

[2] The Fraction after the Prayer and the Prayer during the Fraction

God of truth, make us worthy also of this Communion, and enable our bodies to receive purity and our souls understanding and knowledge. And instruct us, God of compassion, through our participation in the Body and the Blood. For through the Only-begotten [be] to You the glory and the power in [the] Holy Spirit both now and to all the ages of ages. Amen.

[3] Laying on of Hands on the People after the Giving of the Fraction to the Clergy

God of compassion, I extend [my] hand upon this people and pray: extend [Your] hand of truth and give [Your] blessing to this people through Your love of humankind and the surpassing mysteries. Let Your hand of awe and power and chastisement and purity and every holiness bless this people and preserve them for advancement and improvement. Through Your Only-begotten Jesus Christ in [the] Holy Spirit both now and to all the ages of ages. Amen.

σου Ἰησοῦ Χριστοῦ ἐν ἁγίῳ πνεύματι καὶ νῦν καὶ εἰς <τοὺς> σύμπαντας αἰῶνας τῶν αἰώνων. ἀμήν.

[4] Μετὰ τὴν διά<δο>σιν τοῦ λαοῦ εὐχή

Εὐχαριστοῦμέν σοὶ δέσποτα ὅτι ἐσφαλμένους ἐκάλεσας καὶ ἡμαρτηκότας προσεποιήσω καὶ ὑπερτέθεισαι τὴν
Col 2.14 καθ᾽ ἡμῶν ἀπειλήν, φιλανθρωπίᾳ τῇ σῇ συγχωρήσας καὶ τῇ μετανοίᾳ ἀπαλείψας καὶ τῇ πρὸς σὲ γνώσει ἀποβαλών. εὐχαριστοῦμέν σοι ὅτι δέδωκας ἡμῖν κοινωνίαν σώματος καὶ αἵματος. εὐλόγησον ἡμᾶς, εὐλόγησον τὸν λαὸν τοῦτον, ποίησον ἡμᾶς μέρος ἔχειν μετὰ τοῦ σώματος καὶ
1 Cor 10.16 τοῦ αἵματος· διὰ τοῦ μονογενοῦ<ς> σου υἱοῦ δι᾽ οὗ σοῦ ἡ δόξα καὶ τὸ κράτος ἐν ἁγίῳ πνεύματι καὶ νῦν καὶ ἀεὶ καὶ εἰς τοὺς σύμπαντας αἰῶνας τών αἰωνιων. ἀμήν.

[5] Εὐχὴ περὶ τῶν προσφερομένων ἐλαίων καὶ ὑδάτων.

Εὐλογοῦμεν διὰ τοῦ ὀνόματος τοῦ μονογενου<ς> σου Ἰησοῦ Χριστοῦ τὰ κτίσμα<τα> ταῦτα, τὸ ὄνομα τοῦ παθόντος ὀνομάζομεν, τοῦ σταυρωθέντος καὶ ἀναστάντος καὶ καθεζομένου ἐν δεξιᾷ τοῦ ἀγενήτου, ἐπὶ τὸ ὕδωρ καὶ ἐπὶ <τὸ> ἔλαιον τοῦτο· χάρισαι δύναμιν θεραπευτικὴν ἐπὶ τὰ κτίσματα ταῦτα, ὅπως πᾶς πυρετὸς καὶ πᾶν δαιμόνιον καὶ πᾶσα νόσος διὰ τῆς πόσεως καὶ τῆς ἀλείψεως ἀπαλλαγῇ, καὶ γένηται φάρμακον θεραπευτικὸν καὶ φάρμακον ὁλοκληρίας ἡ τῶν κτισμάτων τούτων μετάληψις ἐν ὀνόματι τοῦ

14 εὐχήν L

[4] Prayer after the Distribution to the People

We give You thanks, Master, for You have called the erring and taken notice of those who have sinned, and You set aside the threat against us. You yielded to Your love of humankind, and You wiped it away in repentance and rejected it according to Your own knowledge. We give You thanks because You have given us Communion of the Body and Blood. Bless us, bless this people, make us to have a portion with the Body and the Blood. Through Your Only-begotten Son through whom the glory and the power are Yours in [the] Holy Spirit both now and forever and to all the ages of ages. Amen.

[5] Prayer for Those Offering Oils and Water

We bless these creatures through the name of the Only-begotten Jesus Christ. Upon this water and upon this oil we name the name of the one who suffered, who was crucified and raised up, and who is seated at the right hand of the Uncreated. Graciously give healing power to these creatures so that, through eating and drinking, every fever and every demon and every disease may be cured, and so that the participation of these creatures may become a healing medicine and a medicine of wholeness in the name of Your Only-begotten

μονογενοῦ<ς> σου Ἰησοῦ Χριστοῦ, δι᾽ οὗ σοὶ ἡ δόξα καὶ τὸ κράτος ἐν ἁγίῳ πνεύματι εἰς τοὺς σύμπαντας αἰῶνας τῶν αἰώνων. ἀμήν.

[6] Χειροθεσία μετὰ τὴν εὐλογίαν τοῦ ὕδατος καὶ τοῦ ἐλαίου

Ps 30.6 Φιλάνθρωπε θεὲ τῆς ἀληθείας συμπαραμεινάτω τῷ
1 Cor 10.16 λαῷ τούτῳ ἡ κοινωνία τοῦ σώματος καὶ τοῦ αἵματος· τὰ
σώματα αὐτῶν ζῶντα ἔστω σώματα καὶ αἱ ψυχαὶ αὐτῶν καθαραὶ ἔστωσαν ψυχαί. δὸς τὴν εὐλογίαν ταύτην εἰς τήρησιν τῆς κοινωνίας καὶ εἰς ἀσφάλειαν τῆς γενομένης εὐχαριστίας, καὶ μακάρισον κοινῇ πάντας καὶ ποίησον ἐκλεκτούς· διὰ τοῦ μονογενοῦ<ς> σου Ἰησοῦ Χριστοῦ ἐν ἁγίῳ πνεύματι καὶ νῦν καὶ εἰς τοὺς σύμπαντας αἰῶνας τῶν αἰώνων. ἀμήν.

[7] Ἁγιασμὸς ὑδάτων

Βασιλεῦ καὶ κύριε τῶν ἁπάντων καὶ δημιουργὲ τῶν ὅλων, ὁ πάσῃ τῇ γενητῇ φύσει διὰ τῆς καταβάσεως τοῦ μονογενοῦ<ς> σου Ἰησοῦ Χριστοῦ χαρισάμε<νος> τὴν σωτηρίαν, ὁ λυτρωσάμενος τὸ πλάσμα τὸ ὑπὸ σοῦ δηιουργηθὲν διὰ τῆς ἐπιδημίας τοῦ ἀρρήτου σου λόγου·
Ps 79.15 ἔφιδε νῦν ἐκ τοῦ οὐρανοῦ καὶ ἐπίβλεψον ἐπὶ τὰ ὕδατα
ταῦτα καὶ πλήρωσον αὐτὰ πνεύματος ἁγίου. ὁ ἀρρητός σου λόγος διὰ τῆς ἐπιδημίας ἐν αὐτοῖς γενέσθω καὶ μεταποιησάτω αὐτῶν τὴν ἐνέργειαν καὶ γεννητικὰ αὐτὰ

6 συμπαραβεινάτω W

Jesus Christ, through whom [be] to You the glory and the power to all the ages of ages. Amen.

[6] Laying on of Hands after the Blessing of Water and Oil

Lover of humankind, God of truth, let the Communion of the Body and the Blood remain present to be helpful to this people. Let their bodies be living bodies and their souls pure. Give this blessing for the keeping of the Communion and for the assurance of the Eucharist, which has been made, and bless all in common and make them elect. Through Your Only-begotten Jesus Christ in [the] Holy Spirit both now and to all the ages of ages. Amen.

[7] Sanctification of Waters

King and Lord of all and Creator of all, through the descent of Your Only-begotten Jesus Christ You have graciously given salvation to all created nature. Through the coming of Your inexpressible Word, You have redeemed that which is formed, having been created by You. Look now from heaven and gaze upon these waters and fill them with [the] Holy Spirit. Let Your inexpressible Word come to be in them. Let it change their operation and make them generative, being filled with Your grace, so that the mystery now being accomplished may

κατασκευασάτω πληρούμενα τῆς σῆς χάριτος, ὅπως τὸ 1 Cor 15.10 μυστήριον τὸ νῦν ἐπιτελούμενον μὴ κενὸν εὑρεθῇ ἐν τοῖς ἀναγεννωμένοις ἀλλὰ πληρώσῃ πάντας τοὺς κατιόντας καὶ βαπτιζομένους τῆς θείας χάριτος. φιλάνθρωπε εὐεργέτα φεῖσαι τοῦ σοῦ ποιήματος, σῶσον τὸ ὑπὸ τῆς δεξιᾶς σου πεπο<ι>ημένον κτίσμα, μόρφωσον πάντας τοὺς ἀναγεννωμένους τὴν θείαν καὶ ἄρρητόν σου μορφήν, ὅπως διὰ τοῦ μεμορφῶσθαι καὶ ἀνα<γε>- 2 Thess 1.5 γεννῆσθαι σωθῆναι δυνηθῶσιν καὶ τῆς βασιλείας σου ἀξιωθῆναι. καὶ ὡς κατελθὼν ὁ μονογενής σου λόγος ἐπὶ τὰ ὕδατα τοῦ Ἰορδάνου ἅγια ἀπέδειξεν, οὕτω καὶ νῦν ἐν τούτοις κατερχέσθω καὶ ἅγια καὶ πνευματικὰ ποιησάτω Rom 8.9; 1 Cor 15.50 πρὸς τὸ μηκέτι σάρκα καὶ αἷμα εἶναι τοὺς βαπτιζομένους, ἀλλὰ πνευματικοὺς καὶ δυναμένους προσκυνεῖν σοὶ τῷ ἀγενήτῳ πατρὶ διὰ Ἰησοῦ Χριστοῦ ἐν ἁγίῳ πνεύματι, δι᾽ οὗ σοὶ ἡ δόξα καὶ τὸ κράτος καὶ νῦν καὶ εἰς τοὺς σύμπαντας αἰῶνας τῶν αἰώνων. ἀμήν.

[8] Εὐχὴ ὑπὲρ βαπτιζομένων

Ps 30.6 Παρακαλοῦμέν σε θεὲ τῆς ἀληθείας ὑπὲρ τοῦ δούλου σου τοῦδε καὶ δεόμεθα ὅπως καταξιώσῃς αὐτὸν τοῦ θείου μυστηρίου καὶ τῆς ἀρρήτου σου ἀναγεννήσεως. σοὶ γάρ φιλάνθρωπε νῦν προσφέρεται, σοὶ αὐτὸν ἀνατίθεμεν· χάρισαι αὐτὸν τῇ θείᾳ ταύτῃ ἀναγεννήσει κοινωνῆσαι πρὸς τὸ μηκέτι αὐτὸν ὑπὸ μηδενὸς σκαιοῦ καὶ πονηροῦ ἄγεσθαι ἀλλὰ σοὶ λατρεύειν διαπαντὸς καὶ τὰ σὰ προστάγματα φυλάττειν ὁδηγοῦντος αὐτὸν τοῦ

7 πεπονημένον W

not be found empty in those being born again, but may fill with divine grace all those who go down and are baptized. Lover of humankind, benefactor: spare that which is made by You, save the creature that was made by Your right hand, and mold all who are born again of Your divine and inexpressible form, so that through being formed and born again they may be able to be saved and be made worthy of Your kingdom. And as Your Only-begotten Word, when He descended upon the waters of the Jordan [and] made them holy, so also now let Him descend into these. Let Him make them holy and spiritual in order that those who are baptized may no longer be flesh and blood but spiritual and able to give worship to You, the uncreated Father through Jesus Christ in [the] Holy Spirit, through whom [be] to You the glory and the power both now and unto all the ages of ages. Amen.

[8] Prayer for Those Being Baptized

God of truth, we implore You for this Your servant and pray that You would make him worthy of the divine mystery and Your inexpressible new birth. For to You, lover of humankind, he is now offered; to You we have devoted him. Graciously grant that he may share in this divine new birth so that he may no longer be led by the wicked and evil one but, being guided by Your Only-begotten Word, he may give worship to You always and keep Your commandments. For through Him the glory

μονογενοῦς σου λόγου· ὅτι δι᾽ αὐτοῦ σοὶ ἡ δόξα καὶ τὸ κράτος ἐν τῷ ἁγίῳ πνεύματι καὶ νῦν καὶ εἰς τοὺς σύμπαντας αἰῶνας τῶν αἰώνων. ἀμήν.

[9] Μετὰ τὴν ἀποταγὴν εὐχή

Κύριε παντοκράτορ σφράγισον τὴν συγκατάθεσιν τοῦ δούλου σου τούτου τὴν πρὸς σὲ νῦν γεγενημένην καὶ ἀμετάβλητον αὐτοῦ τὸ ἦθος καὶ τὸν τρόπον διαφύλαξον, ἵνα μηκέτι τοῖς χείροσιν ὑπηρετῇ ἀλλ᾽ ἐν τῷ τῆς ἀλη-
Ps 30.6 θείας θεῷ λατρεύῃ καὶ σοι τῷ τῶν πάντων ποιητῇ δουλεύῃ πρὸς τὸ τέλειον αὐτὸν καί σοι γνήσιον ἀποδειχθῆναι· διὰ τοῦ μονογενοῦς σου Ἰησοῦ Χριστοῦ, δι᾽ οὗ σοὶ ἡ δόξα καὶ τὸ κράτος ἐν ἁγίῳ πνεύματι καὶ νῦν καὶ εἰς τοὺς σύμπαντας αἰῶνας τῶν αἰώνων. ἀμήν.

[10] Μετὰ τὴν ἀνάληψιν εὐχή

Φιλάνθρωπε εὐεργέτα σωτὴρ πάντων τὴν ἐπιστροφὴν πρὸς σὲ πεποιημένων, ἵλεως γενοῦ τῷ δούλῳ σου τῷδε· ὁδήγησον αὐτὸν ἐπὶ τὴν ἀναγέννησιν τῇ δεξιᾷ σου. ὁ μονογενής σου λόγος ὁδηγείτω αὐτὸν ἐπὶ τὸ λουτρόν· τιμηθήτω αὐτοῦ ἡ ἀναγέννησις, μὴ ἔστω κενὴ τῆς σῆς
2 Cor 6.1 χάριτος· συμπαρίτω ὁ ἅγιός σου λόγος, συνέστω τὸ ἅγιόν σου πνεῦμα ἀποσοβοῦν καὶ ἀποβάλλον πάντα πειρασμόν· ὅτι διὰ τοῦ μονογενοῦς σου Ἰησοῦ Χριστοῦ

1 σκαιοῦ A F : κακοῦ W | 8 χήροσιν A W | 8 B suggests adding either ἀλλὰ σοὶ or ἀλλ᾽ ἐν τῷ πνεύματι here. | 14 ἀνάληψιν A F W : ἄλειψιν B | 20 συμπαρεῖτω A

and the power [be] to You in the Holy Spirit both now and to all the ages of ages. Amen.

[9] Prayer after the Renunciation

Almighty Lord, seal the assent of this Your servant that has now been made before You. Keep his custom and way unchangeable so that, no longer serving those who are worse, he may offer worship to the God of truth and serve You, the Creator of all, and may be made perfect and legitimate to You. Through Your Only-begotten Jesus Christ, through whom [be] to You the glory and the power in [the] Holy Spirit both now and unto all the ages of ages. Amen.

[10] Prayer after the Reception[2]

Lover of humankind, benefactor, Savior of all who have made conversion toward You, be merciful to this Your servant. Guide him to the new birth with Your right hand. Let Your Only-begotten Word guide him to the bath. Let his new birth be honored; let it not be empty of Your grace. Let Your holy Word be present and let Your Holy Spirit be with him to drive away and cast out every temptation. For, through Your Only-begotten Jesus Christ the glory and the power [be] to You both now and to all the ages of ages. Amen.

[2] Or, "Anointing," if, with B, ἄλειψιν is the preferred reading.

<σοὶ> ἡ δόξα καὶ τὸ κράτος καὶ νῦν καὶ εἰς τοὺς σύμπαντας αἰῶνας τῶν αἰώνων. ἀμήν.

[11] Μετὰ τὸ βαπτισθῆναι καὶ ἀνελθεῖν εὐχή

Ps 30.6 Ὁ θεὸς ὁ τῆς ἀληθείας θεός, ὁ τῶν πάντων δημιουργός,
ὁ κύριος πάσης τῆς κτίσεως, εὐλόγησον τὸν δοῦλόν
σου τοῦτον εὐλογίᾳ τῇ σῇ· καθαρὸν αὐτὸν δεῖξον ἐν
τῇ ἀναγεννήσει, κοινιωνὸν αὐτὸν ταῖς ἀγγελικαῖς σου
δυνάμεσιν κατάστησον, ἵνα μηκέτι σὰρξ ἀλλὰ πνευμα-
Rom 8.9 τικὸς ὀνομάζηται μετασχὼν τῆς θείας σου καὶ ὠφελίμου
δωρεᾶς· διατηρηθείη μέχρι τέλους σοὶ τῷ τῶν ὅλων ποι-
ητῇ· διὰ τοῦ μονογενοῦς σου Ἰησοῦ Χριστοῦ, δι᾽ οὗ σοὶ
ἡ δόξα καὶ τὸ κράτος ἐν ἁγίῳ πνεύματι καὶ νῦν καὶ εἰς
τοὺς σύμπαντας αἰῶνας τῶν αἰώνων. ἀμήν.

[12] Χειροθεσία καταστάσεως Διακόνων

Jn 3.16–17 Πάτερ τοῦ μονογενοῦς ὁ τὸν υἱόν σου ἀποστείλας
καὶ διατάξας τὰ ἐπὶ τῆς γῆς πράγματα καὶ κανόνας τῇ
ἐκκλησίᾳ καὶ τάξεις δεδιωκὼς εἰς ὠφέλειαν καὶ σωτηρίαν τῶν ποιμνίων, ὁ ἐκλεξάμενος ἐπισκόπους καὶ πρε-
σβυτέρους καὶ διακόνους εἰς λειτουργίαν τῆς καθολικῆς
σου ἐκκλησίας, ὁ ἐκλεξάμενος διὰ τοῦ μονογενοῦς σου
Acts 6.1–6 τοὺς ζ΄ διακόνους καὶ χαρισάμενος αὐτοῖς πνεῦμα ἅγιον·
κατάστησον καὶ τόνδε διάκονον τῆς καθολικῆς σου
Is 11.2; 1 Cor 12.10 ἐκκλησίας καὶ δὸς ἐν αὐτῷ πνεῦμα γνώσεως καὶ διακρί-
σεως, ἵνα δυνηθῇ μεταξὺ τοῦ λαοῦ τοῦ ἁγίου καθαρῶς

3 Εὐχ A | 9 φελίμου A | 21 ζ΄ A : ἑπτά F W

[11] Prayer after Being Baptized and Coming Up

God, the God of truth and Creator of all, the Lord of every creature, bless this Your servant with Your blessing. Show him pure in the new birth. Place him in communion with Your angelic powers so that he may no longer be called flesh but spiritual, having a share of Your divine and beneficial gift. May he be preserved until the end for You, the Maker of all. Through Your Only-begotten Jesus Christ, through whom [be] to You the glory and the power in [the] Holy Spirit both now and unto all the ages of ages. Amen.

[12] Laying on of Hands for the Appointment of Deacons

Father of the Only-begotten, You sent Your Son and ordered the events upon earth. You gave canons and orders to the Church for the advantage and salvation of the flocks. You elected bishops and presbyters and deacons for the service of Your catholic Church. Through Your Only-begotten You elected the seven deacons and graciously gave [the] Holy Spirit to them. Appoint also this one a deacon of Your catholic Church. Graciously give him a spirit of knowledge and discernment that he may be able to minister purely and blamelessly in this service in the midst of Your holy people. Through Your Only-begotten Jesus Christ, through whom [be] to You

καὶ ἀμέμπτως διακονῆσαι ἐν τῇ λειτουργίᾳ ταύτῃ· διὰ τοῦ μονογενοῦς σου Ἰησοῦ Χριστοῦ, δι᾽ οὗ σοὶ ἡ δόξα καὶ τὸ κράτος ἐν ἁγίῳ πνεύματι καὶ νῦν καὶ εἰς τοὺς σύμπαντας αἰῶνας τῶν αἰώνων. ἀμήν.

[13] Χειροθεσία καταστάσεως Πρεσβυτέρων

2 Esd 1.5 Τὴν χεῖρα ἐκτείνομεν δέσποτα θεὲ τῶν οὐρανῶν πάτερ
τοῦ μονογενοῦς σου ἐπὶ τὸν ἄνθρωπον τοῦτον καὶ δεό-
Jn 15.26 μεθα ἵνα τὸ πνεῦμα τῆς ἀληθείας ἐπιδημήσῃ αὐτῷ· φρόνησιν αὐτῷ χάρισαι καὶ γνῶσιν καὶ καρδίαν ἀγαθήν·
γενέσθω ἐν αὐτῷ πνεῦμα θεῖον πρὸς τὸ δύνασθαι αὐτὸν
οἰκονομῆσαι τὸν λαόν σου καὶ πρεσβεύειν τὰ θεῖά σου
2 Cor 5.20 λόγια καὶ καταλλάξαι τὸν λαόν σου σοὶ τῷ ἀγενήτῳ θεῷ.
ὁ χαρισάμενος ἀπὸ τοῦ πνεύματος τοῦ Μωσέως ἐπὶ τοὺς
Num 11.16–25 ἐκλελεγμένους πνεῦμα ἅγιον, μέρισον καὶ τῷδε πνεῦμα
ἅγιον ἐκ τοῦ πνεύματος τοῦ μονογενοῦς εἰς χάριν
1 Cor 12.8–9 σοφίας καὶ γνώσεως καὶ πίστεως ὀρθῆς, ἵνα δυνηθῇ σοι
1 Tim 3.9; 2 Tim 1.3 ὑπηρετῆσαι ἐν καθαρᾷ συνειδήσει· διὰ τοῦ μονογενοῦς
σου Ἰησοῦ Χριστοῦ, δι᾽ οὗ σοὶ ἡ δόξα καὶ τὸ κράτος ἐν
ἁγίῳ πνεύματι καὶ νῦν καὶ εἰς τοὺς σύμπαντας αἰῶνας
τῶν αἰώνιων. ἀμήν.

[14] Χειροθεσία καταστάσεως Ἐπισκόπου

Ὁ τὸν κύριον Ἰησοῦν ἀποστείλας εἰς κέρδος ὅλης τῆς
Jn 3.17 | Lk 6.13 οἰκουμένης, ὁ δι᾽ αὐτοῦ τοὺς ἀποστόλους ἐκλεξάμενος, ὁ

1 ἀμέμπστως A | 11 οἰκονομῖσαι A | 17 ὑπηρεῆσαι A | 17 συνΐδησει A

the glory and the power in [the] Holy Spirit both now and to all the ages of ages. Amen.

[13] Laying on of Hands for the Appointment of Presbyters

Master, God of the heavens, Father of Your Only-begotten, we extend [our] hand[s] upon this man and we pray that the Spirit of truth may come to him. Graciously give him insight and knowledge and a good heart. Let [the] divine Spirit come to be in him that he might be able to govern Your people, to act as an ambassador of Your divine words, and to reconcile Your people to You, the uncreated God. From the spirit of Moses You graciously gave [the] Holy Spirit to the elect. Distribute [the] Holy Spirit also to this one from the Spirit of the Only-begotten for the gift of wisdom and knowledge and right faith, that he may be able to serve You with a pure conscience. Through Your Only-begotten Jesus Christ, through whom [be] to You the glory and the power in [the] Holy Spirit both now and to all the ages of ages. Amen.

[14] Laying on of Hands for the Appointment of the Bishop

God of truth, You sent the Lord Jesus for the benefit of the whole world. Through him You elected the apostles, appointing holy bishops from generation to generation. Make this one also a living bishop, a holy bishop

Esth 9.27 κατὰ γενεὰν καὶ γενεὰν ἐπισκόπους ἁγίους χειροτονῶν·
Ps 30.6 ποίησον ὁ θεὸς τῆς ἀληθείας καὶ τόνδε ἐπίσκοπον ζῶντα,
ἐπίσκοπον ἅγιον τῆς διαδοχῆς τῶν ἁγίων ἀποστόλων,
καὶ δὸς αὐτῷ χάριν καὶ πνεῦμα θεῖον, ὅ ἐχαρίσω πᾶσιν
τοῖς γνησίοις σου δούλοις καὶ προφήταις καὶ πατριάρ-
χαις· ποίησον αὐτὸν ἄξιον εἶναι ποιμαίνειν σου τὴν ποί-
Acts 20.28; 1 Pet 5.2 μνην ἔτι τε ἀμέμπτως καὶ ἀπροσκόπως ἐν τῇ ἐπισκοπῇ
διατελείτω· διὰ τοῦ μονογενοῦς σου Ἰησοῦ Χριστοῦ, δι᾽
οὗ σοὶ ἡ δόξα καὶ τὸ κράτος ἐν ἁγίῳ πνεύματι καὶ νῦν καὶ
εἰς τοὺς σύμπαντας αἰῶνας τῶν αἰώνων. ἀμήν.

Προσευχ Σαραπίωνος θμούεως·

[15] Εὐχὴ εἰς τὸ Ἄλειμμα τῶν βαπτιζομένων

Wis 11.26 Δέσποτα φιλάνθρωπε καὶ φιλόψυχε, οἰκτίρμον καὶ ἐλε-
Ps 85.15 | Ps 30.6 ῆμον, <θεὲ> τῆς ἀληθείας, ἐπιλαλούμεθά σε ἐξακολου-
θοῦντες καὶ πειθόμενοι ταῖς ἐπαγγελίαις τοῦ μονογε-
νοῦς σου εἰρηκότος Ἐάν τινων ἀφῆτε τὰς ἁμαρτίας ἀφί-
Jn 20.23 ενται αὐτοῖς· καὶ ἀλείφομεν τῷ ἀλείμματι τούτῳ τοὺς
προς<ιόν>τας ἢ προσιούσας τῇ θείᾳ ταύτῃ ἀναγεννήσει,
παρακαλοῦντες ὥστε τὸν κύριον ἡμῶν Χριστὸν Ἰησοῦν
ἐνεργῆσαι αὐτῷ ἰατικὴν καὶ ἰσχυροποιητικὴν δύναμιν
καὶ ἀποκαλύψαι μὲν διὰ τοὺς ἀλείμματος τούτου καὶ
ἀποθεραπεῦσαι ἀπὸ ψυχῆς σώματος πνεύματος αὐτῶν
πᾶν σημεῖον ἁμαρτίας καὶ ἀνομίας ἢ σατανικῆς αἰτίας,
τῇ δὲ ἰδίᾳ χάριτι τὴν ἄφεσιν αὐτοῖς παρασχέσθαι, ἵνα

3 B suggests ἄξιον | 7 ἀπροσκόπτως A | 11 Προσευχ A : Προσευχὴ W | 11 θμούσεως | 12 Εὐχ A | 19 προστάσει προσιούσας A : προθέσει προσιόντας W : προσιόντας ἢ τὰς προσιούσας F | 20 αὐτοῖς W

of the succession of the apostles, and give to him grace and [the] divine Spirit, which You graciously gave to all of Your genuine servants and prophets and patriarchs. Make him worthy to shepherd Your flock and let him continue both blamelessly and without stumbling in the episcopate. Through Your Only-begotten Jesus Christ, through whom [be] to You the glory and the power in [the] Holy Spirit both now and to all the ages of ages. Amen.

Prayer of Sarapion of Thmuis

[15] Prayer for the Oil of Those Being Baptized

Master, lover of humankind and lover of souls, compassionate and merciful, God of truth, we call upon You, following and obeying the promises of Your Only-begotten, who has said, "If you forgive the sins of any they are forgiven them." And we anoint with this oil those who approach this divine rebirth, imploring that our Lord Christ Jesus may work in this oil and reveal healing and strength-producing power through it,[3] and may heal their soul, body, spirit from every sign of sin and lawlessness or satanic taint, and by his own grace may grant forgiveness to them so that, having no part in sin, they will live in righteousness. And, when they have been molded again through this oil and purified through the bath and

[3]Or, "imploring that healing and strength-producing power may work in it and reveal our Lord Christ Jesus through this oil ..."

1 Pet 2.24 τῇ ἁμαρτίᾳ ἀπογενόμενοι τῇ δικαιοσύνῃ ζήσουσι καὶ
διὰ τῆς ἀλείψεως ταύτης ἀναπλασθέντες καὶ διὰ τοῦ
Tit 3.5; Eph 5.26 λουτροῦ καθαρισθέντες καὶ τῷ πνεύματι ἀνανεωθέντες ἐξισχύσουσιν κατανικῆσαι λοιπὸν τὰς προσβαλ-
λούσας αὐτοῖς ἀντικειμένας ἐνεργείας καὶ ἀπάτας τοῦ
βίου τούτου καὶ οὕτως συνδεθῆναι καὶ συνενωθῆναι τῇ
2 Pet 3.18 ποίμνῃ τοῦ κυρίου καὶ σωτῆρος ἡμῶν Ἰησοῦ Χριστοῦ
Rom 8.17; Eph 3.6; Heb 11.9 καὶ συγκληρονομῆσαι τοῖς ἁγίοις τὰς ἐπαγγελίας· ὅτι δι᾽
αὐτοῦ <σοὶ> ἡ δόξα καὶ τὸ κράτος ἐν ἁγίῳ πνεύματι εἰς
τοὺς σύμπαντας αἰῶνας τῶν αἰώνων. ἀμήν.

[16] Εὐχὴ εἰς τὸ χρίσμα ἐν ᾧ χρίονται οἱ βαπισθέντες

Ps 79.8 Ὁ θεὸς τῶν δυνάμεων ὁ βοηθὸς πάσης ψυχῆς ἐπιστρε-
1 Pet 5.6 φούσης ἐπὶ σὲ καὶ γινομένης ὑπὸ τὴν κραταίαν σου χεῖρα
τοῦ μονογενοῦς, ἐπικαλούμεθά σε, ὥστε διὰ τῆς θείας
2 Pet 1.3 καὶ ἀοράτου σου δυνάμεως τοῦ κυρίου καὶ σωτῆρος
ἡμῶν Ἰησοῦ Χριστοῦ ἐνεργῆσαι ἐν τῷ χρίσματι τούτῳ
ἐνέργειαν θείαν καὶ οὐράνιον, ἵνα οἱ βαπτισθέντες καὶ
χριόμενοι ἐν αὐτῷ τὸ ἐκτύπωμα τοῦ σημείου τοῦ σωτη-
ριώδους σταυροῦ τοῦ μονογενοῦς, δι᾽ οὗ σταυροῦ διε-
τράπη καὶ ἐθριαμβεύθη σατανᾶς καὶ πᾶσα δύναμις ἀντι-
Col 2.15 κειμένη, ὡς ἀναγεννηθέντες καὶ ἀνανεωθέντες διὰ τοῦ
Tit 3.5 λουτροῦ τῆς παλιγγενεσίας καὶ οὗτοι μέτοχοι γένωνται
Acts 2.38, 10.45 τῆς δωρεᾶς τοῦ ἁγίου πνεύματος καὶ ἀσφαλισθέντες τῇ
1 Cor 15.58 σφραγῖδι ταύτῃ διαμείνωσιν ἑδραῖοι καὶ ἀμετακίνητοι,

11 Εὐχ A | 19 Σωτηρίου δοὺς A | 22 γινένωνται A

renewed in the Spirit, they will be strong enough to conquer against other opposing works and deceits of this life that come near them, and so be bound and united to the flock of our Lord and Savior Jesus Christ and inherit the promises to the saints. For through Him [be] to You the glory and the power in [the] Holy Spirit unto all the ages of ages. Amen.

[16] Prayer for the Chrism with Which the Baptized Are Anointed

God of powers, the Helper of every soul who turns to You and comes under the powerful hand of Your Only-begotten, we implore You that, through the divine and inexpressible power of our Lord and Savior Jesus Christ, divine and heavenly energy may work in this chrism, so that those who have been baptized and are anointed by it, with the impression of the sign of the saving cross of the Only-begotten, the cross through which Satan and all opposing powers were overthrown and triumphed over,[4] as those having been reborn and renewed through

[4]This phrase presents grammatical difficulties. Something like μετά (*meta*) must be supplied if the above translation is to be correct. However, if the reading supplied by A (σωτηρίου δούς, *sōtēriou dous*) is correct, then this phrase can be translated: "...so that those who have been baptized and are anointed, having given in it the impression of the sign of salvation, [the] cross of the Only-begotten, the cross through which Satan was overthrown..." Another possibility is

ἀβλαβεῖς καὶ ἄσυλοι, ἀνεπηρέαστοι καὶ ἀνεπιβούλευτοι, ἐμπολιτευόμενοι ἐν τῇ πίστει καὶ ἐπιγνώσει τῆς ἀληθείας μέχρι τέλους, ἀναμένοντες τὰς οὐρανίους τῆς ζωῆς ἐλπίδας καὶ αἰωνίους ἐπαγγελία<ς> τοῦ κυρίου καὶ σωτῆρος ἡμῶν Ἰησοῦ Χριστοῦ, δι᾽ οὗ σοὶ ἡ δόξα καὶ τὸ κράτος ἐν ἁγίῳ πνεύματι καὶ νῦν καὶ εἰς τοὺς σύμπαντας αἰῶνας τῶν αἰώνων. ἀμήν.

2 Thess 2.13; 1 Tim 2.4 | Tit 1.2, 3.7

2 Pet 2.20, 3.18

[17] Εὐχὴ εἰς ἔλαιον νοσούντων ἢ εἰς ἄρτον ἢ εἰς ὕδωρ

Ἐπικαλούμεθα σὲ τὸν ἔχοντα πᾶσαν ἐξουσίαν καὶ δύναμιν τὸν σωτῆρα πάντων ἀνθρώπων, πατέρα τοῦ κυρίου ἡμῶν καὶ σωτῆρος Ἰησοῦ Χριστοῦ, καὶ δεόμεθα ὥστε ἐκπέμψαι δύναμιν ἰατικὴν ἀπὸ τῶν οὐρανῶν τοῦ μονογενοῦς ἐπὶ τὸ ἔλαιον τοῦτο, ἵνα γένηται τοῖς χριομένοις ἢ μεταλαμβάνουσιν τῶν κτισμάτων σου τούτων εἰς ἀποβολὴν πάσης νόσου καὶ πάσης μαλακίας, εἰς ἀλεξιφάρμακον παντὸς δαιμονίου, εἰς ἐκχωρισμὸν παντὸς πνεύματος ἀκαθάρτου, εἰς ἀφορισμὸν παντὸς πνεύματος πονηροῦ, εἰς ἐκδιωγμὸν παντὸς πυρετοῦ καὶ ῥίγους καὶ πάσης ἀσθενείας, εἰς χάριν ἀγαθὴν καὶ ἄφεσιν ἁμαρτημάτων, εἰς φάρμακον ζωῆς καὶ σωτηρίας, εἰς ὑγείαν καὶ ὁλοκληρίαν ψυχῆς σώματος πνεύματος, εἰς ῥῶσιν τελείαν. φοβηθήτω δέσποτα πᾶσα ἐνέργεια σατανική, πᾶν δαιμόνιον, πᾶσα ἐπιβουλὴ τοῦ ἀντικειμένου, πᾶσα

1 Tim 4.10

2 Cor 1.3; 2 Pet 2.20, 3.18

Mt 4.23, 9.35, 10.1

1 Thess 5.23

8 Εὐχ A | 18 ὑγίαν

the washing of regeneration, they may also become sharers of the gift of the Holy Spirit and, having been sealed in this seal, may remain firm and immovable, without harm and safe from violence, free from insult and unassailable, dwelling in the faith and knowledge of the truth until the end, in expectation of the hopes of heavenly life and the eternal promises of our Lord and Savior Jesus Christ, through whom [be] to You the glory and the power in [the] Holy Spirit both now and forever. Amen.

[17] Prayer for Oil of the Sick or for Bread or for Water

Father of our Lord and Savior Jesus Christ, having all authority and power, the Savior of all people, we call

---

that the entire phrase is a clumsy interpolation added to explain the meaning of the ritual gesture used in the act of anointing. If so, then σωτηριόδους could have been the original reading, which the eleventh-century copyist, unable to find either a verb or suitable preposition elsewhere in the text, logically read as a contraction of σωτηρίου and δούς.

Furthermore, if this phrase is omitted the text reads rather smoothly: "So that those who have been baptized and are anointed by it, as those having been reborn and renewed through the washing of regeneration, may also become sharers of the gift of the Holy Spirit, and, having been sealed in this seal, may remain firm and immovable..." Without this sign of the cross phrase a close parallel in construction and sequence appears in Prayer 15: "So that, having no part of sin, they will live in righteousness. And when they have been molded again through this anointing and purified through the bath and renewed in the Spirit, they will be strong enough..."

πληγή, πᾶσα μάστιξ, πᾶσα ἀλγηδών, πᾶς πόνος ἤ ῥάπισμα ἤ ἐντίναγμα ἤ σκίασμα πονηρὸν τὸ ὄνομά σου τὸ ἅγιον, ὅ ἐπεκαλεσάμεθα νῦν ἡμεῖς, καὶ τὸ ὄνομα τοῦ μονογενοῦς, καὶ ἀπερχέσθωσαν ἀπὸ τῶν ἐντὸς <καὶ> τῶν ἐκτὸς τῶν δούλων σου τούτων· ἵνα δοξασθῇ τὸ ὄνομα τοῦ ὑπὲρ ἡμῶν σταυρωθέντος καὶ ἀναστάντος (Mt 8.17) τοῦ τὰς νόσους ἡμῶν καὶ τὰς ἀσθενείας ἀναλαβόντος Ἰησοῦ Χρισοῦ καὶ ἐρχομένου κρῖναι ζῶντας καὶ νεκρούς· ὅτι δι᾽ αὐτοῦ σοὶ ἡ δόξα καὶ τὸ κράτος ἐν ἁγίῳ πνεύματι καὶ νῦν καὶ εἰς τοὺς σύμπαντας αἰῶνας τῶν αἰώνων. ἀμήν.

[18] Εὐχὴ περὶ τεθνεῶντος καὶ ἐκκομιζομένου

(Wis 16.13) Ὁ θεὸς ὁ ζωῆς καὶ θανάτου τὴν ἐξουσίαν ἔχων, ὁ θεὸς τῶν πνευμάτων καὶ δεσπότης πάσης σαρκός, ὁ θεὸς ὁ θανατῶν καὶ ζωογονῶν, ὁ κατάγων εἰς πύλας ᾅδου

2 ἐντείναγμα W | 3 ἐπικαλεσάμεθα A | 24 Εὐχ A

upon You and we implore You that the healing power of Your Only-begotten may be sent out from heaven upon this oil. May it become to those who are anointed [*or* to those who receive of these Your creatures] for a rejection of every disease and every sickness, for an amulet warding off every demon, for a departing of every unclean spirit, for a taking away of every evil spirit, for a driving away of all fever and shiverings and every weakness, for good grace and forgiveness of sins, for a medicine of life and salvation, for health and wholeness of soul, body, spirit, for perfect strength. Master, let every satanic energy, every demon, every plot of the opposing one, every blow, every lash, every pain, or every slap in the face, or shaking, or evil shadow be afraid of Your holy name, which we have now called upon, and the name of the Only-begotten; and let them depart from the inner and the outer parts of these Your servants so that the name of Jesus Christ, the one who was crucified and rose for us, who took to Himself our diseases and weaknesses, and is coming to judge the living and the dead, may be glorified. For through Him [be] to You the glory and the power in [the] Holy Spirit both now and to all the ages of ages. Amen.

[18] Prayer for One Who Has Died and Is Being Carried Out

God, You have the power of life and death, God of the spirits and Master of all flesh, God of the dead and of the living. You lead down to the doors of Hades and You lead up. You create the human spirit in a person and take the

καὶ ἀνάγων, ὁ κτίζων πνεῦμα ἀνθρώπου ἐν αὐτῷ καὶ
Wis 16.13–14; παραλαμβάνων τῶν ἁγίων τὰς ψυχὰς καὶ ἀναπαύων· ὁ
Num 16.22; 1 Kgs 2.6 ἀλλοιῶν καὶ μεταβάλλων καὶ μετασχηματίζων τὰ κτίσματά σου καθὼς δίκαιον καὶ σύμφορόν ἐστιν, μόνος
1 Tim 1.17 αὐτὸς ἄφθαρτος καὶ ἀναλλοίωτος καὶ αἰώνιος ὤν· δεόμεθά σου περὶ τῆς κοιμήσεως καὶ ἀναπαύσεως τοῦ δούλου σου τοῦδε ἢ τῆς δούλης σου τῆσδε· τὴν ψυχήν, τὸ
Ps 22.2 πνεῦμα αὐτοῦ ἀνάπαυσον ἐν τόποις χλόης, ἐν ταμείοις ἀναπαύσεως μετὰ Ἀβραὰμ καὶ Ισαὰκ καὶ ᾿Ιακὼβ καὶ
Mt 8.11; Lk 13.28 πάντων τῶν ἁγίων σου, τὸ δὲ σῶμα ἀνάστησον ἐν ᾗ
Jn 6.40, 44, 54| Tit 1.2 ὥρισας ἡμέρᾳ κατὰ τὰς ἀψευδεῖς σου ἐπαγγελίας, ἵνα καὶ τὰς κατ᾽ ἀξίαν αὐτῷ κληρονομίας ἀποδῶς ἐν ταῖς ἁγίαις σου νομαῖς. τῶν παραπτωμάτων αὐτοῦ καὶ ἁμαρ-
Ps 24.7 | 2 Pet 1.15 τημάτων μὴ μνησθῇς, τὴν δὲ ἔξοδον αὐτοῦ εἰρηνικὴν καὶ εὐλογημένην εἶναι ποίησον· τὰς λύπας τῶν διαφερόντων πνεύματι παρακλήσεως ἴασαι καὶ ἡμῖν πᾶσι τέλος ἀγαθὸν δώρησαι· διὰ τοῦ μονογενοῦς σου Ἰησοῦ Χριστοῦ, δι᾽ οὗ σοὶ ἡ δόξα καὶ τὸ κράτος ἐν ἁγίῳ πνεύματι εἰς τοὺς αἰῶνας τῶν αἰώνων. ἀμήν.

[19] Εὐχὴ Πρώτη Κυριακῆς

Παρακαλοῦμεν σὲ τὸν πατέρα τοῦ μονογενοῦς, τὸν κύριον τοῦ παντός, τὸν δημιουργὸν τῶν κτισμάτων, τὸν ποιητὴν τῶν πεποιημένων· καθαρὰς ἐκτείνομεν τὰς χεῖρας καὶ τὰς διανοίας ἀναπετάννυμεν πρὸς σὲ κύριε· δεόμεθα, οἴκτειρον φεῖσαι εὐεργέτησον βελτίωσον, πλη-
Ps 105.4 θυνον ἐν ἀρετῇ καὶ πίστει καὶ γνώσει· ἐπίσκεψαι ἡμᾶς κύριε, πρὸς σὲ τὰς ἀσθενείας ἑαυτῶν ἀναπέμπομεν·

souls of the saints and give them rest. You, who alone are incorruptible and unchangeable and eternal, are the one who changes and turns and transforms Your creatures as it is right and beneficial. We pray to You for the sleep and rest of this Your servant or of this Your handmaid. Give rest to his soul, his spirit, in green pastures, in the inner rooms of rest with Abraham, Isaac, and Jacob and all Your saints. And raise [his] body on the appointed day according to Your truthful promises so that You may give to him according to the worthy inheritance[s] in Your holy pastures. Do not remember his transgressions and his sins, but make his departure to be peaceful and blessed. Heal the grief of those who carry [him] with a spirit of consolation and give us all a good end. Through Your Only-begotten Jesus Christ, through whom [be] to You the glory and the power in [the] Holy Spirit to the ages of ages. Amen.

[19] First Prayer of the Lord's Day

We implore You, the Father of the Only-begotten, the Lord of all, the Creator of all created things, the Maker of what has been made. We stretch out pure hands and we open [our] minds toward You, Lord. We pray: have compassion on us, spare us, benefit us, make us better, make us increase in virtue and in faith and in knowledge. Visit us Lord, to You we send up our own weaknesses. Be

ἱλάσθητι καὶ ἐλέησον κοινῇ πάντας ἡμᾶς· ἐλέησον τὸν λαὸν τοῦτον, εὐεργέτησον, ἐπιεικῆ καὶ σώφρονα καὶ καθαρὸν ποίησον, καὶ δυνάμεις ἀγγελικὰς ἀπόστειλον, ἵνα ὁ λαός σου οὗτος ἅπας ἅγιος καὶ σεμνὸς ᾖ. παρακαλῶ δὲ πνεῦμα ἅγιον ἀπόστειλον εἰς τὴν ἡμετέραν διάνοιαν καὶ χάρισαι ἡμῖν μαθεῖν τὰς θείας γραφὰς ἀπὸ ἁγίου πνεύματος καὶ διερμηνεύειν καθαρῶς καὶ ἀξίως, ἵνα ὠφεληθῶσιν οἱ παρόντες λαοὶ πάντες· διὰ τοῦ μονογενοῦς σου Ἰησοῦ Χριστοῦ ἐν ἁγίῳ πνεύματι, δι᾽ οὗ σοὶ ἡ δόξα καὶ τὸ κράτος καὶ νῦν καὶ εἰς τοὺς σύμπαντας αἰῶνας τῶν αἰώνων. ἀμήν.

[20] Μετὰ τὸ Ἀναστῆναι ἀπὸ τῆς Ὁμιλίας Εὐχή

Ps 26.9 Ὁ θεὸς ὁ σωτήρ, ὁ θεὸς τοῦ παντός, ὁ τῶν ὅλων κύριος καὶ δημιουργός, ὁ γεννήτωρ τοῦ μονογενοῦς, ὁ τὸν
Heb 1.3 χαρακτῆρα τὸν ζῶντα καὶ ἀληθινὸν γεννήσας, ὁ πρὸς ὠφέλειαν τοῦ γένους τῶν ἀνθρώπων αὐτὸν ἀποστείλας, ὁ δι᾽ αὐτοῦ καλέσας καὶ προσποιησάμενος τοὺς ἀνθρώπους· δεόμεθά σου ὑπὲρ τοῦ λαοῦ τούτου· πνεῦμα ἅγιον πέμψον καὶ ὁ κύριος Ἰησοῦς ἐπισκεψάσθω, λαλησάτω ἐν ταῖς διανοίαις πάντων καὶ προοικονομησάτω εἰς πίστιν τὰς καρδίας· αὐτὸς πρὸς σὲ ἑλκυσάτω τὰς ψυχὰς θεὲ τῶν οἰκτιρμῶν· κτῆσαι λαὸν καὶ ἐν τῇ πόλει ταύτῃ, κτῆσαι ποίμνιον γνήσιον· διὰ τοῦ μονογενοῦς σου Ἰησοῦ Χριστοῦ ἐν ἁγίῳ πνεύματι, δι᾽ οὗ σοὶ ἡ δόξα καὶ τὸ κράτος καὶ νῦν καὶ εἰς τοὺς σύμπαντας αἰῶνας τῶν αἰώνων. ἀμήν.

5 δὲ A : σε W F | 12 Εὐχ A | 22 κτῆσαι A F : κτίσαι W

merciful and have mercy upon us all in common. Have mercy on this people, make them better, gentle and prudent and pure, and send angelic powers in order that this whole people may be holy and noble. And, I implore You, send [the] Holy Spirit into our mind and graciously help us to learn the divine writings from [the] Holy Spirit and to interpret[5] them purely and worthily, so that all the people present may be aided. Through Your Only-begotten Jesus Christ in [the] Holy Spirit, through whom [be] to You the power and the glory both now and unto all the ages of ages. Amen.

[20] Prayer after the Standing Up from the Homily

God, the Savior of all, the God of all, the Lord and Creator of all, the Begetter of the Only-begotten, You begat the living and true image, [and] You sent him for the advantage of the human race. Through Him You called and claimed the peoples. We pray to You for this Your people. Send [the] Holy Spirit and let the Lord Jesus visit. Let Him speak in all minds and let Him build up all hearts in faith. Let Him draw all souls to You, God of compassion. Acquire a people, acquire a genuine flock also in this city. Through Your Only-begotten Jesus Christ in [the] Holy Spirit, through whom [be] to You the glory and the power both now and unto all the ages of ages. Amen.

[5] Or "translate."

[21] Εὐχὴ ὑπὲρ τῶν Κατηχουμένων

Βοηθὲ καὶ κύριε τῶν ἁπάντων, ἐλευθερωτὰ τῶν ἐλευθε-
ρωθέντων, προστάτα τῶν ῥυσθέντων, ἡ ἐλπὶς τῶν ὑπὸ
1 Pet 5.6 τὴν κραταίαν σου χεῖρα γεγονότων· σὺ εἶ ὁ τὴν ἀνο-
μίαν καθῃρηκώς, ὁ διὰ τοῦ μονογενοῦς καταργήσας
Heb 2.14; 1 Jn 3.8 τὸν σατανᾶν καὶ λύσας αὐτοῦ τὰ τεχνάσματα καὶ ἀπο-
Lk 13.16 λύσας τοὺς ὑπ᾽ αὐτοῦ δεδεμένους· εὐχαριστοῦμέν σοι
ὑπὲρ τῶν κατηχουμένων, ὅτι κέκληκας αὐτοὺς διὰ τοῦ
μονογενοῦς καὶ γνῶσιν αὐτοῖς τὴν σὴν ἐχαρίσω· καὶ διὰ
τοῦτο δεόμεθα, βεβαιωθήτιωσαν ἐν τῇ γνώσει, ἵνα γινώ-
σκωσιν σὲ τὸν μόνον ἀληθινὸν θεὸν καὶ ὃν ἀπέστειλας
Jn 17.3 Ἰησοῦν Χριστόν· διαφυλαττέσθωσαν ἐν τοῖς μαθήμασιν
καὶ ἐν τῇ καθαρᾷ φρονήσει καὶ προκοπτέτωσαν ἄξιοι
Tit 3.5 γενέσθαι τοῦ λουτροῦ τῆς παλιγγενεσίας καὶ τῶν ἁγίων
μυστηρίων· διὰ τοῦ μονογενοῦς Ἰησοῦ Χριστοῦ ἐν ἁγίῳ
πνεύματι, δι᾽ οὗ σοὶ ἡ δόξα καὶ τὸ κράτος καὶ νῦν καὶ εἰς
τοὺς σύμπαντας αἰῶνας τῶν αἰώνων. ἀμήν.

[22] Εὐχὴ περὶ Νοσούντων

Παρακαλοῦμεν σὲ τὸν ἔφορον καὶ κύριον καὶ πλάστην τοῦ σώματος καὶ ποιητὴν τῆς ψυχῆς, τὸν ἁρμοσάμενον τὸν ἄνθρωπον, τὸν οἰκονόμον καὶ κυβερνήτην καὶ σωτῆρα παντὸς τοὺς γένους τῶν ἀνθρώπων, τὸν καταλ<λ>ασσόμενον καὶ πραϋνόμενον διὰ τὴν ἰδίαν φιλανθρωπίαν· ἱλάσθητι δέσποτα· βοήθησον καὶ ἴασαι

1 Εὐχ A | 5 χεῖραν A | 10 Γινώσκουσιν A | 26 βοήθησαι AW

[21] Prayer for the Catechumens

Helper and Lord of all, deliverer of those who have been set free, champion of those who have been delivered, the hope of those who have come under Your powerful hand. You are the one who has put down lawlessness, who, through Your Only-begotten, has made Satan powerless and destroyed his handiworks, and released those who were bound by him. We give thanks to You for the catechumens, for You have called them through Your Only-begotten and graciously given them Your knowledge. And, on account of this we pray: let them be established in knowledge so that they may know You the only true God and Jesus Christ whom You sent. Let them be guarded in the teachings and in a pure understanding; and let them progress to become worthy of the washing of regeneration and the holy mysteries. Through Your Only-begotten Jesus Christ in [the] Holy Spirit, through whom [be] to You the glory and the power both now and unto all the ages of ages. Amen.

[22] Prayer for the Sick

We implore You the overseer and Lord and molder of the body and maker of the soul. You are the one who fit humankind together. You are the manager and pilot and Savior of the descendants of humankind, and the one who is reconciled and made gentle through Your own love of humankind. Be merciful, Master. Help and heal all who are sick. Rebuke the diseases. Raise those who

πάντας τοὺς νοσοῦντας. ἐπιτίμησον τοῖς νοσήμασιν· [Lk 4.39; Jas 5.16] ἀνάστησον τοὺς κατακειμένους· δὸς δόξαν τῷ ὀνόματί [Ps 113.9] σοῦ τῷ ἁγίῳ διὰ τοῦ μονογενοῦς σου Ἰησοῦ Χριστοῦ, δι᾽ οὗ σοὶ ἡ δόξα καὶ τὸ κράτος ἐν ἁγίῳ πνεύματι καὶ νῦν καὶ εἰς τοὺς σύμπαντας αἰῶνας τῶν αἰώνων. ἀμήν.

[23] Εὐχὴ ὑπὲρ Καρποφορίας

Οὐρανοῦ καὶ γῆς δημιουργέ, ὁ τὸν οὐρανὸν διὰ τοῦ χοροῦ τῶν ἀστέρων στεφανώσας καὶ διὰ τῶν φωστήρων λαμπρύνας, ὁ τὴν γῆν τοῖς καρποῖς τιμήσας πρὸς ὠφέλειαν τῶν ἀνθρώπων, ὁ χαρισάμενος τῷ γένει τῷ ὑπό σου πεπλασμένῳ ἄνωθεν μὲν ἀπολαύειν τῆς αὐγῆς καὶ τοῦ φωτὸς τῶν φωστήρων, κάτωθεν δὲ τρέφεσθαι ἀπὸ τῶν καρπῶν τῆς γῆς· δεόμεθα χάρισαι τοὺς ὑετοὺς πληρεστάτους καὶ γονιμωτάτους· ποίησον δὲ καὶ τὴν γῆν καρποφορῆσαι καὶ πολλὴν ἐνέγκαι εὐφορίαν ἕνεκεν τῆς [Tit 3.4] σῆς φιλανθρωπίας καὶ χρηστότητος· μνήσθητι τῶν σὲ ἐπικαλουμένων, τίμησον τὴν ἁγίαν σου καὶ μόνην καθολικὴν ἐκκλησίαν καὶ εἰσάκουσον τῶν παρακλήσεων καὶ τῶν προσευχῶν ἡμῶν καὶ εὐλόγησον τὴν γῆν πᾶσαν· διὰ τοῦ μονογενοῦς σου Ἰησοῦ Χριστοῦ, δι᾽ οὗ σοὶ ἡ δόξα καὶ τὸ κράτος ἐν ἁγίῳ πνεύματι καὶ νῦν καὶ εἰς τοὺς σύμπαντας αἰῶνας τῶν αἰώνων. ἀμήν.

6 Εὐχ A | 11 χρησάμενος…πεπλαιμένω AW

are lying down. Give glory to Your holy name through Your Only-begotten Jesus Christ, through whom [be] to You the glory and the power in [the] Holy Spirit both now and unto all the ages of ages. Amen.

[23] Prayer for Fruit-bearing

Creator of heaven and earth, You crowned heaven through the choir of stars and brightened it through the luminaries, and You honored the earth with fruits for the benefit of the peoples. You graciously gave to the generation that was formed by You both to enjoy the dawn and the light of the luminaries above, and to be fed from the fruits of the earth below. We pray, graciously send the most filling and most fertilizing rains, and also make the earth produce fruit and bear a great crop for the sake of Your love of humankind and generosity. Remember those who call upon You. Honor Your holy and only catholic Church and hear our supplications and prayers and bless all the earth. Through Your Only-begotten Jesus Christ, through whom [be] to You the glory and the power in [the] Holy Spirit both now and unto all the ages of ages. Amen.

[24] Εὐχὴ περὶ τῆς Ἐκκλησίας

Sir 36.17 | Num 16.22 Κύριε θεὲ τῶν αἰώνων, θεὲ τῶν λογικῶν πνευμάτων, θεὲ ψυχῶν καθαρῶν καὶ πάντων τῶν γνησίως σε καὶ καθαρῶς ἐπικαλουμένων, ὁ ἐν οὐρανῷ φαινόμενος καὶ γινωσκόμενος τοῖς καθαροῖς πνεύμασιν, ὁ ἐπὶ γῆς ὑμνούμενος καὶ κατοικῶν ἐν τῇ καθολικῇ ἐκκλησίᾳ, ὑπὸ ἀγγέλων ἁγίων λειτουργούμενος καὶ καθαρῶν ψυχῶν, ὁ ποιήσας καὶ ἐξ οὐρανῶν χορὸν ζῶντα εἰς δόξαν καὶ αἶνον τῆς ἀληθείας· δὸς τὴν ἐκκλησίαν ταύτην ζῶσαν καὶ καθαρὰν ἐκκλησίαν εἶναι, δὸς αὐτὴν ἔχειν θείας δυνάμεις καὶ καθαροὺς ἀγγέλους λειτουργούς, ἵνα δυνηθῇ καθαρῶς ὑμνεῖν σε. παρακλοῦμεν ὑπὲρ πάντων ἀνθρώπων τῆς ἐκκλησίας ταύτης· πᾶσιν καταλλάγηθι, πᾶσιν συγχώρησον, πᾶσιν ἄφεσιν ἁμαρτημάτων δός· χάρισαι μηκέτι μηδὲν ἁμαρτάνειν, ἀλλὰ γενοῦ τεῖχος αὐτοῖς καὶ κατάργησον πάντα πειρασμόν. ἐλέησον ἄνδρας καὶ γυναῖκας καὶ παιδία καὶ φάνηθι ἐν πᾶσιν καὶ γραφήτω σου ἡ γνῶσις ἐν ταῖς καρ-
Heb 8.10–11 δίαις αὐτῶν· διὰ τοῦ μονογενοῦς σου Ἰησοῦ Χριστοῦ, δι᾽ οὗ σοὶ ἡ δόξα καὶ τὸ κράτος ἐν ἁγίῳ πνεύματι καὶ νῦν καὶ εἰς τοὺς σύμπαντας αἰῶνας τῶν αἰώνων. ἀμήν.

[25] Εὐχὴ ὑπὲρ Ἐπισκόπου καὶ τῆς Ἐκκλησίας

Σὲ τὸν σωτῆρα καὶ κύριον ἐπικαλούμεθα, τὸν θεὸν πάσης σαρκὸς καὶ κύριον παντὸς πνεύματος, τὸν εὐλογητὸν
Num 16.22 καὶ χορηγὸν πάσης εὐλογίας· ἁγίασον τὸν ἐπίσκοπον

1 Εὐχ A| 21 Εὐχ A | 24 χορητὸν A

[24] Prayer for the Church

Lord God of ages, God of rational spirits, God of pure souls and of all who call upon You genuinely and purely, You shine in heaven and are known to the pure spirits, You are hymned upon earth and dwell in the catholic Church, You are served by angels and pure souls, and You also made a living chorus from heaven for the glory and praise of truth. Grant that this church may be a living and pure church. Grant that it may be given divine power and pure serving angels, so that it may be able to hymn You purely. We implore You for all people of this church: be reconciled to all, give remission to all, give forgiveness of sins to all. Graciously grant that they may not sin anymore, but be a wall to them and make all temptation powerless. Have mercy on men and women and children. And be revealed in all and let Your knowledge be written in their hearts. Through Your Only-begotten Jesus Christ, through whom [be] to You the glory and the power in [the] Holy Spirit both now and unto all the ages of ages. Amen.

[25] Prayer for the Bishop and the Church

We call upon You the Savior and Lord, the God of all flesh and the Lord of every spirit, the blesser and supplier of every blessing. Sanctify this bishop and keep him from every temptation and give him wisdom and knowledge,

τόνδε καὶ διατήρησον αὐτὸν ἔξω παντὸς πειρασμοῦ καὶ δὸς αὐτῷ σοφίαν καὶ γνῶσιν, εὐόδωσον αὐτὸν ἐν ταῖς σαῖς ἐπιστήμαις. παρακαλοῦμεν δὲ καὶ ὑπὲρ τῶν συμπρεσβυτέρων, ἁγίασον αὐτούς, σοφίαν αὐτοῖς δὸς καὶ γνῶσιν καὶ ὀρθὴν διδασκαλίαν· ποίησον αὐτοὺς πρεσβεύειν τὰς ἁγίας σου διδασκαλίας ὀρθῶς καὶ ἀμέμπτως. ἁγίασον δὲ καὶ διακόνους, ἵνα ὦσιν καθαροὶ καρδίᾳ καὶ σώματι καὶ δυνηθῶσιν καθαρᾷ συνειδήσει Mt 5.8 λειτουργεῖν καὶ παραστῆναι τῷ ἁγίῳ σώματι καὶ τῷ 1 Tim 3.9; ἁγίῳ αἵματι. Παρακαλοῦμεν δὲ ὑπὲρ τῶν ὑποδιακόνων 2 Tim 1.3 καὶ ἀναγνωστῶν καὶ ἑρμηνέων· πάντας τοὺς τῆς ἐκκλησίας <λειτουργοὺς> ἀνάπαυσον καὶ πᾶσιν δὸς ἔλεος καὶ οἰκτιρμὸν καὶ προκοπήν. δεόμεθα ὑπὲρ τῶν μοναζόντων καὶ ὑπὲρ τῶν παρθενευουσῶν· τελεσάτωσαν τὸν δρόμον ἑαυτῶν ἀμέμπτως καὶ τὸν βίον ἑαυτῶν ἀδιαλείπτως, ἵνα δυνηθῶσιν ἐν καθαρότητι διατρῖψαι καὶ ἁγιότητι τὰς ἡμέρας ἑαυτῶν πάσας. ἐλέησον δὲ καὶ τοὺς γεγαμηκό- Lk 1.75 τας πάντας, τοὺς ἄνδρας καὶ τὰ γύναια καὶ τὰ παιδία, καὶ δὸς πᾶσιν εὐλογίαν προκοπῆς καὶ βελτιώσεως, ἵνα πάντες γένωνται ζῶντες καὶ ἐκλεκτοὶ ἄνθρωποι. διὰ τοῦ μονογενοῦς σου Ἰησοῦ Χριστοῦ, δι᾽ οὗ σοὶ ἡ δόξα καὶ τὸ κράτος ἐν ἁγίῳ πνεύματι καὶ νύν καὶ εἰς τοὺς αἰῶνας τῶν αἰώνων. ἀμήν.

6 <τοὺς> διακόνους F | 13 παρθερθευουσῶν A : παρθένον εὖ οὐσῶν W

and success in his disciplines. And we implore You also for the co-presbyters: sanctify them, give them wisdom and knowledge and right teaching. Make them to represent Your holy teachings rightly and purely. And sanctify also the deacons so that they may be pure in heart and body and may be able to serve with a pure conscience and to stand by the holy Body and the holy Blood. And we implore You for the subdeacons and readers and interpreters: refresh all the ministers of the Church and give mercy and compassion and advancement to all. We pray to You for the monks and for the virgins: let them finish their course blamelessly and their life unceasingly so that they may be able to spend all their days in the highest purity and holiness. And have mercy also on all who are married, the men and women and children, and give to all a blessing of advancement and improvement, so that all may become living and elect people. Through Your Only-begotten Jesus Christ, through whom [be] to You the glory and the power in [the] Holy Spirit both now and unto all the ages of ages. Amen.

[26] Εὐχὴ γονυκλισίας

Ps 85.15 Πάτερ τοῦ μονογενούς, ἀγαθὲ καὶ οἰκτίρμον, ἐλεῆμον καὶ
Wis 11.26 φιλάνθρωπε καὶ φιλόψυχε, εὐεργέτα πάντων, τῶν ἐπὶ
σὲ ἐπιστρεφόντων, δέχου τὴν παράκλησιν ταύτην καὶ
δὸς ἡμῖν γνῶσιν καὶ πίστιν καὶ εὐσέβειαν καὶ ὁσιότητα.
κατάργησον πᾶν πάθος, πᾶσαν ἡδονήν, πᾶσαν ἁμαρτίαν
ἀπὸ τοῦ λαοῦ τούτου· ποίησον πάντας γενέσθαι καθα-
ρούς· συγχώρησον πᾶσιν τὰ πλημμελήματα. σοὶ γὰρ τῷ
ἀγενήτῳ πατρὶ διὰ τοῦ μονογενοῦς κλίνομεν τὸ γόνυ,
δὸς ἡμῖν νοῦν ὅσιον καὶ τελείαν ὠφέλειαν, δὸς ἡμᾶς σὲ
Acts 17.27 ζητεῖν καὶ ἀγαπᾶν, δὸς ἡμῖν ἐρευνᾶν καὶ ἐκζητεῖν τὰ θεία
Eph 3.5 σου λόγια, δὸς ἡμῖν χεῖρα δέσποτα καὶ ἀνάστησον ἡμᾶς·
ἀνάστησον ὁ θεὸς τῶν οἰκτιρμῶν, ποίησον ἀναβλέπειν·
ἀνακάλυψον ἡμῶν τοὺς ὀφθαλμούς, παρρησίαν ἡμῖν
χάρισαι, μὴ ἐπιτρέψῃς ἡμᾶς αἰσχύνεσθαι μηδὲ δυσω-
πεῖσθαι μηδὲ καταγινώσκειν ἑαυτῶν· ἐξάλειψον τὸ καθ'
Col 2.14 ἡμών χειρόγραφον, γράψον ἡμῶν τὰ ὀνόματα ἐν βιβλίῳ
Rev 13.8 ζωῆς, συναρίθμησον ἡμᾶς τοῖς ἁγίοις σου προφήταις καὶ
Eph 3.5 ἀποστόλοις· διὰ τοῦ μονογενοῦς σου Ἰησοῦ Χριστοῦ, δι'
οὗ σοὶ ἡ δόξα καὶ τὸ κράτος ἐν ἁγίῳ πνεύματι καὶ νῦν καὶ
εἰς τοὺς σύμπαντας αἰῶνας τῶν αἰώνων. ἀμήν.

[27] Εὐχὴ ὑπὲρ Λαοῦ

Ἐξομολογούμεθά σοι φιλάνθρωπε θεὲ καὶ προσρίπτομεν ἑαυτῶν τὰς ἀσθενείας καὶ δύναμιν ἡμῖν προσγενέσθαι

15 ἐπιστρέψης A | 22 Εὐχ A | 23 ἐξενεγκὼν A W

[26] Prayer of Genuflection

Father of the Only-begotten, good and compassionate, merciful and lover of humankind and lover of souls, benefactor of all who turn to You, receive this request and give us knowledge and faith and piety and devoutness. Abolish every passion, every lust, every sin from this people. Make all of them pure. Forgive all of them their faults. For to You, the uncreated Father, through the Only-begotten we bend the knee. Give us a devout mind and perfect assistance. Grant that we may seek and love You. Grant that we may search and seek out Your divine words. Give us a hand, Master, and raise us up. God of compassion, raise us up and make us look up. Unveil our eyes. Graciously give us freedom of speech. Do not allow us to be ashamed, nor to be troubled, nor to condemn ourselves. Wipe away the bond against us. Write our names in the book of life and number us with Your holy prophets and apostles. Through Your Only-begotten Jesus Christ, through whom [be] to You the glory and the power in [the] Holy Spirit both now and unto all the ages of ages. Amen.

[27] Prayer for the People

We confess to You, God, lover of humankind, and we cast before You our weaknesses and implore You for power to be added to us. Grant forgiveness for sins that have been added, and forgive all errors that have

παρακαλοῦμεν. σύγγνωθι τοῖς προγεγενημένοις ἁμαρτήμασιν καὶ ἄφες πάντα τὰ παρῳχημένα σφάλματα [Eph 4.24] καὶ ποίησον καινοὺς ἀνθρώπους. δεῖξον ἡμᾶς καὶ δούλους γνησίους καὶ καθαρούς. σοὶ ἀνατίθεμεν ἑαυτούς, [Ps 30.6] δέχου ἡμᾶς θεὲ τῆς ἀληθείας, δέχου τὸν λαὸν τοῦτον· δὸς ὅλον γνήσιον γενέσθαι, δὸς ὅλον ἀμέμπτως καὶ καθαρῶς πολιτεύεσθαι. συμμετρηθήτωσαν τοῖς οὐρανίοις, συναριθμηθήτωσαν τοῖς ἀγγέλοις, ὅλοι ἐκλεκτοὶ καὶ ἅγιοι γενέσθωσαν. παρακαλοῦμέν σε ὑπὲρ τῶν πεπιστευκότων καὶ τὸν κύριον Ἰησοῦν Χριστὸν ἐπεγνωκότων, βεβαιωθήτωσαν ἐν τῇ πίστει καὶ τῇ γνώσει καὶ τῇ [Col 2.7] διδασκαλίᾳ. δεόμεθα ὑπὲρ παντὸς τοῦ λαοῦ τούτου, καταλλάγηθι πᾶσιν, γνώρισον ἑαυτόν, ἀποκάλυψόν σου τὸ φέγγος· γνώτωσάν σε πάντες τὸν ἀγένητον πατέρα [Jn 17.3] καὶ τὸν μονογενῆ σου υἱὸν Ἰησοῦν Χριστόν. δεόμεθα ὑπὲρ πάντων ἀρχόντων, εἰρηνικὸν τὸν βίον ἐχέτωσαν [1 Tim 2.2] ὑπὲρ ἀναπαύσεως τῆς καθολικῆς ἐκκλησίας. δεόμεθα θεὲ τῶν οἰκτιρμῶν ὑπὲρ ἐλευθέρων καὶ δούλων, ἀρρένων καὶ γυναικῶν, γερόντων καὶ παιδίων, πενήτων καὶ πλουσίων· πᾶσιν τὸ ἴδιόν σου δεῖξον χρηστὸν καὶ τὴν [Tit 3.5] ἰδίαν σου πᾶσιν πρότεινον φιλανθρωπίαν· πάντας οἰκτειρον καὶ πᾶσιν χάρισαι τὴν πρὸς σὲ ἐπιστροφήν. παρακαλοῦμεν ὑπὲρ ἀποδημούντων, χάρισαι αὐτοῖς ἄγγελον εἰρηνικὸν συνοδοιπόρον γενέσθαι, ἵνα μηδὲν ὑπὸ μηδενὸς ζημιωθῶσιν, ἵνα ἐν πολλῇ εὐθυμίᾳ τὸν πλοῦν καὶ τὰς ἀποδημίας αὐτῶν διανύσωσιν. παρακαλοῦμεν ὑπὲρ τεθλιμμένων καὶ δεδεμένων καὶ πενήτων·

25 μηδένα A W

passed by and make us new people. Make us also legitimate and pure servants. To You we have dedicated ourselves. Receive us, God of truth. Receive this people. Grant that they may become entirely genuine and live entirely blamelessly and purely. Let them be numbered among the heavenly ones, counted among the angels, and let them be entirely elect and holy. We implore You for those who have believed and who have known the Lord Jesus Christ: let them be confirmed in the faith and in the knowledge and in the teaching. We pray to You for all of this people: be reconciled to all, make Yourself known, reveal Your radiance. Let all know You the uncreated Father and Your Only-begotten Son Jesus Christ. We pray for all rulers: let them have a peaceful life for the sake of the rest of the catholic Church.[6] We pray, God of mercies, for the free and the slaves, for males and females, old people and children, rich and poor. Show to all Your own kindness and spread out to all Your own love of humankind. Have compassion on all and graciously give to all conversion to You. We implore You for those who are traveling: graciously give them a peaceful angel as a co-traveler so that they may not be injured by anyone and may complete their voyage and their journeys with much cheer. We implore You, the comforter and consoler, for those who are oppressed

[6]Wordsworth, 90, translates this as two separate petitions, one for the peaceful life of rulers and one for the rest of the catholic Church. While this may be possible on the basis of the repetition of ὑπέρ (*hyper*), the lack of a separate verb of prayer as well as a probable allusion to 1 Timothy 2.2 suggests that it is not the case.

ἀνάπαυσον ἕκαστον, ἀπάλλαξον δεσμῶν, ἐξένεγκον τῆς πενίας, παρηγόρησον πάντας ὁ παρηγορῶν καὶ παραμυθούμενος. δεόμεθα ὑπὲρ νοσούντων, ὑγείαν χάρισαι καὶ τῆς νόσου ἀνάστησον καὶ ποίησον αὐτοὺς τελείαν ἔχειν ὑγείαν σώματος καὶ ψυχῆς. σὺ γὰρ εἶ ὁ σωτὴρ καὶ εὐεργέτης, σὺ εἶ ὁ πάντων κύριος καὶ βασιλεύς· σὲ παρακεκλήκαμεν ὑπὲρ πάντων διὰ τοῦ μονογενοῦς σου Ἰησοῦ Χριστοῦ, δι᾽ οὗ σοὶ ἡ δόξα καὶ τὸ <κράτο>ς ἐν ἁγίῳ πνεύματι καὶ νῦν καὶ εἰς τοὺς σύμπαντας αἰῶνας τῶν αἰώνων. ἀμήν.

[28] Χειροθεσία κατηχουμένων

Τὴν χεῖρα ἐκτείνομεν δέσποτα καὶ δεόμεθα τὴν χεῖρα τὴν θείαν καὶ ζῶσαν ἐκταθῆναι εἰς εὐλογίαν τῷ λαῷ τούτῳ· σοὶ γαρ ἀγένητε πάτερ διὰ τοῦ μονογενοῦς κεκλίκασιν τὰς κεφαλάς· εὐλόγησον τὸν λαὸν τοῦτον εἰς εὐλογίαν γνώσεως καὶ εὐσεβείας, εἰς εὐλογίαν τῶν σῶν μυστηρίων· διὰ τοῦ μονογενοῦς σου Ἰησοῦ Χριστοῦ, δι᾽ οὗ σοὶ ἡ δόξα καὶ τὸ κράτος ἐν ἁγίῳ πνεύματι καὶ νῦν καὶ εἰς τοὺς σύμπαντας αἰῶνας τῶν αἰώνων. ἀμήν.

[29] Χειροθεσία λαϊκῶν

Ἡ ζῶσα καὶ καθαρὰ χείρ, ἡ χεὶρ τοῦ μονογενοῦς, ἡ πάντα τὰ πονηρὰ καθῃρηκυῖα καὶ πάντα τὰ ἅγια βεβαιώσασ<α> καὶ ἠσφαλισμένη, ἐκταθήτω ἐπὶ τὰς κεφαλὰς τοῦ λαοῦ

1 ἐξομολογούμεσθα A

and those who are bound and those who are poor: give rest to each of them, release them from bonds, lead them out of poverty, and comfort them all. We pray for the sick: graciously give them health and raise them from sickness and make them to have perfect health of body and soul. For You are the Savior and benefactor, You are the Lord and king of all. And we have implored You for all through Your Only-begotten Jesus Christ, through whom [be] to You the glory and the power in [the] Holy Spirit both now and unto all the ages of ages. Amen.

[28] Laying on of Hands on Catechumens

We stretch out [our] hand, Master, and we pray: stretch out the divine and living hand in blessing to this people. For to You, the uncreated Father, through the Only-begotten, they have bowed the heads. Bless this people for a blessing of knowledge and piety, for a blessing of Your mysteries. Through Your Only-begotten Jesus Christ, through whom [be] to You the glory and the power in [the] Holy Spirit both now and to all the ages of ages. Amen.

[29] Laying on of Hands on the People

Let the living and pure hand, the hand of the Only-begotten, which has destroyed all evil things and has confirmed and safeguarded all holy things, be extended upon the heads of this people. Let this people be blessed

τούτου· εὐλογηθείη ὁ λαὸς οὗτος εὐλογία πνεύματος, εὐλογία οὐρανοῦ, εὐλογία προφητῶν καὶ ἀποστόλων· εὐλογηθείη τὰ σώματα τοῦ λαοῦ εἰς σωφροσύνην καὶ καθαρότητα· εὐλογηθείσησαν αἱ ψυχαὶ αὐτῶν εἰς μάθησιν καὶ γνῶσιν καὶ τὰ μυστήρια· εὐλογηθείσησαν κοινῇ πάντες· διὰ τοῦ μονογενοῦς σου Ἰησοῦ Χριστοῦ, δι᾽ οὗ σοὶ ἡ δόξα καὶ τὸ κράτος ἐν ἁγίῳ πνεύματι καὶ νῦν καὶ εἰς τοὺς σύμπαντας αἰῶνας <τῶν> αἰώνων. ἀμήν.

[30] Χειροθεσία νοσούντων

Κύριε θεὲ τῶν οἰκτιρμῶν ἔκτεινόν σου τὴν χεῖρα καὶ χάρισαι θεραπευθῆναι τοὺς νοσοῦντας πάντας· χάρισαι τῆς ὑγείας ἀξιωθῆναι, ἀπάλλαξον αὐτοὺς τῆς ἐπικειμένης νόσου· ἐν τῷ ὀνόματι τοῦ μονογενοῦς σου θεραπευθήτωσαν, γενέσθω αὐτοῖς φάρμακον τὸ ἅγιον αὐτοῦ ὄνομα εἰς ὑγείαν καὶ ὁλοκληρίαν· ὅτι δι᾽ αὐτοῦ σοι ἡ δόξα καὶ τὸ κράτος ἐν ἁγίῳ πνεύματι καὶ νῦν καὶ εἰς τοὺς σύμπαντας αἰῶνας τῶν <αἰ>ιώνων. ἀμήν.

Πᾶσαι αὗται εὐχαὶ ἐπιτελοῦνται πρὸ τῆς εὐχῆς τοῦ προσφόρου.

18 εὐχῆς τοῦ are covered by a flaw in A

with blessing of [the] Spirit, with blessing of heaven, with blessing of prophets and apostles. Let their bodies be blessed for self-control and purity. Let their souls be blessed for learning and knowledge and the mysteries. Let all be blessed in common. Through Your Only-begotten Jesus Christ, through whom [be] to You the glory and the power in [the] Holy Spirit both now and to all the ages of ages. Amen.

[30] Laying on of Hands on the Sick

Lord God of compassion, stretch out Your hand and graciously grant healing to all the sick. Graciously make them worthy of health. Release them from the sickness that lies upon them. Let them be healed in the name of Your Only-begotten. Let His holy name come to be in them a medicine for health and wholeness. For through Him [be] to You the glory and the power in [the] Holy Spirit both now and to all the ages of ages. Amen.

All these prayers are accomplished before the Prayer of Offering.

POPULAR PATRISTICS SERIES

1 *On the Priesthood* – St John Chrysostom
6 *On the Holy Icons* – St Theodore the Studite
7 *On Marriage and Family Life* – St John Chrysostom
8 *On the Divine Liturgy* – St Germanus
9 *On Wealth and Poverty* – St John Chrysostom
10 *Hymns on Paradise* – St Ephrem the Syrian
11 *On Ascetical Life* – St Isaac of Nineveh
12 *On the Soul and Resurrection* – St Gregory of Nyssa
13 *On the Unity of Christ* – St Cyril of Alexandria
14 *On the Mystical Life*, vol. 1 – St Symeon the New Theologian
15 *On the Mystical Life*, vol. 2 – St Symeon the New Theologian
16 *On the Mystical Life*, vol. 3 – St Symeon the New Theologian
17 *On the Apostolic Preaching* – St Irenaeus
18 *On the Dormition* – Early Patristic Homilies
19 *On the Mother of God* – Jacob of Serug
21 *On God and Man* – Theological Poetry of St Gregory of Nazianzus
23 *On God and Christ* – St Gregory of Nazianzus
24 *Three Treatises on the Divine Images* – St John of Damascus
25 *On the Cosmic Mystery of Christ* – St Maximus the Confessor
26 *Letters from the Desert* – Barsanuphius and John
27 *Four Desert Fathers* – Coptic Texts
28 *Saint Macarius the Spiritbearer* – Coptic Texts
29 *On the Lord's Prayer* – Tertullian, Cyprian, Origen
30 *On the Human Condition* – St Basil the Great
31 *The Cult of the Saints* – St John Chrysostom
32 *On the Church: Select Treatises* – St Cyprian of Carthage
33 *On the Church: Select Letters* – St Cyprian of Carthage
34 *The Book of Pastoral Rule* – St Gregory the Great
35 *Wider than Heaven* – Homilies on the Mother of God
36 *Festal Orations* – St Gregory of Nazianzus
37 *Counsels on the Spiritual Life* – Mark the Monk
38 *On Social Justice* – St Basil the Great
39 *The Harp of Glory* – An African Akathist
40 *Divine Eros* – St Symeon the New Theologian
41 *On the Two Ways* – Foundational Texts in the Tradition
42 *On the Holy Spirit* – St Basil the Great
43 *Works on the Spirit* – Athanasius and Didymus
44 *On the Incarnation* – St Athanasius
45 *Treasure-House of Mysteries* – Poetry in the Syriac Tradition
46 *Poems on Scripture* – St Gregory of Nazianzus
47 *On Christian Doctrine and Practice* – St Basil the Great
48 *Light on the Mountain* – Homilies on the Transfiguration
49 *The Letters* – St Ignatius of Antioch
50 *On Fasting and Feasts* – St Basil the Great
51 *On Christian Ethics* – St Basil the Great
52 *Give Me a Word* – The Desert Fathers
53 *Two Hundred Chapters on Theology* – St Maximus the Confessor
54 *On the Apostolic Tradition* – Hippolytus
55 *On Pascha* – Melito of Sardis
56 *Letters to Olympia* – St John Chrysostom
57 *Lectures on the Christian Sacraments* – St Cyril of Jerusalem
58 *The Testament of the Lord*
59 *On the Ecclesiastical Mystagogy* – St Maximus the Confessor
60 *Catechetical Discourse* – St Gregory of Nyssa
61 *Hymns of Repentance* – St Romanos the Melodist
62 *On the Orthodox Faith* – St John of Damascus
63 *Headings on Spiritual Knowledge* – Isaac of Nineveh
64 *On Death and Eternal Life* – St Gregory of Nyssa
65 *The Prayers of Saint Sarapion* – Saint Sarapion of Thmuis

We hope this book has been enjoyable and edifying for your spiritual journey toward our Lord and Savior Jesus Christ.

One hundred percent of the net proceeds of all SVS Press sales directly support the mission of St Vladimir's Orthodox Theological Seminary to train priests, lay leaders, and scholars to be active apologists of the Orthodox Christian Faith. However, the proceeds only partially cover the operational costs of St Vladimir's Seminary. To meet our annual budget, we rely on the generosity of donors who are passionate about providing theological education and spiritual formation to the next generation of ordained and lay servant leaders in the Orthodox Church.

Donations are tax-deductible and can be made at
www.svots.edu/give.
We greatly appreciate your generosity.

To engage more with St Vladimir's Orthodox
Theological Seminary, please visit:

www.svots.edu
online.svots.edu
www.svspress.com
www.instituteofsacredarts.com

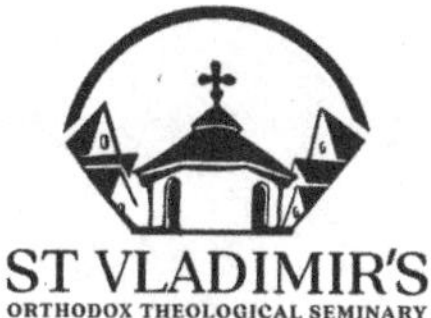